DISCARDED

STATESMEN OF THE
OLD SOUTH

THE MACMILLAN COMPANY
NEW YORK · BOSTON · CHICAGO · DALLAS
ATLANTA · SAN FRANCISCO

MACMILLAN & CO., Limited
LONDON · BOMBAY · CALCUTTA
MELBOURNE

**THE MACMILLAN COMPANY
OF CANADA, Limited**
TORONTO

STATESMEN OF THE OLD SOUTH

―― OR ――

FROM RADICALISM TO CONSERVATIVE REVOLT

BY

WILLIAM E. DODD, Ph.D.

PROFESSOR OF AMERICAN HISTORY IN
THE UNIVERSITY OF CHICAGO

NEW YORK
THE MACMILLAN COMPANY
1929

COPYRIGHT, 1911,
By THE MACMILLAN COMPANY.

All rights reserved, including
the right of reproduction in
whole or in part in any form.

Set up and electrotyped. Published September, 1911.
Reissued January, 1926. Reprinted November, 1929;
December, 1929.

PRINTED IN THE UNITED STATES OF AMERICA
BY BERWICK & SMITH CO.

Lamar College

To My Father

PREFACE

THE substance of the following papers has been presented in the form of popular lectures at the University of California, the University of Indiana, the University of Chicago, Richmond and Randolph Macon Colleges and it cannot be expected that the treatment of these interesting Southern leaders of the olden time will be found entirely free from the defects of the lecture method. Still it is hoped that the point of view and the interpretation of certain facts and conditions of the Southern and national evolution may justify the publication of these studies.

The author is under obligations to Mr. C. D. Johns, of the University of Chicago, for reading the entire proof and for making the index.

WM. E. DODD.

University of Chicago
July 20, 1911

CONTENTS

Preface vii

Thomas Jefferson 1

John C. Calhoun 91

Jefferson Davis 171

Index 239

FROM RADICALISM TO CONSERVATIVE REVOLT

STATESMEN OF THE OLD SOUTH

THOMAS JEFFERSON

I

THOMAS JEFFERSON is a name to conjure with in the United States. Extreme individualists who desire to exploit the resources of the nation and re-establish feudalism in the world, make pious pilgrimages to Monticello; radical democrats who feel that the principles of the Declaration of Independence are about to perish from the earth, regard the great Virginia leader as their patron saint; and socialists appeal to the writings of Jefferson for grave opinions to justify the "régime of the future." Andrew Jackson overturned the old Jefferson party in the name of its founder and Abraham Lincoln based his arguments against slavery upon well-known passages from the famous *Notes on*

Virginia, while Jefferson Davis believed from the bottom of his heart that secession and civil war, even on behalf of slavery, was only an application of the doctrine of the Virginia and Kentucky resolutions! And Jefferson himself gave reason for many of these divergent and irreconcilable views; in his published writings there is abundant justification for the contentions of these present-day followers, though the man, were he still with us, would speedily repudiate any and all who deny the full and complete application of the doctrine of democracy, that is the democracy of Lincoln as against slavery, of Bryan as against Wall street, of the West as against the East. Jefferson would have been a populist in 1892 or an insurgent in 1910.

"Jefferson, the populist." With this rather startling idea in mind, let us look into the life of the "Man of the Mountain," as John Randolph was accustomed to say.

Peter Jefferson, the father of Thomas, was a westerner, a land surveyor and Indian fighter, a character not unlike that of Daniel Boone, vigorous, rough, close-fisted. The colony of Virginia employed him to survey her southern boundary line and like most other surveyors of land he patented a good deal for himself and settled upon it during the fourth decade of the eighteenth century to "grow up with the back-country." He came into such good standing with Isham Randolph of Dungeness that he was given one of the daughters, of whom there were usually many among the great clans of Virginia, to wife. Thomas was therefore well born, though no aristocrat. The young boy was put to school with a Scotch pedagogue in Louisa county—the home at that time of radical democracy and hard-headed Presbyterian dissent. But the schooling was good and the environment better in view of the coming career of the boy. In Louisa county men wore buckskin breeches, Indian moccasins and hunting shirts without coats to cover them, crowned with coonskin caps. There was still much hunting of deer and turkeys among the hills and mountains of Louisa—the fine country made famous a hundred years later by the marches of Lee and Jackson and the two great battles at Manassas—and a slender stooping youth from neighboring Hanover had already made a name for himself in that region by his "long hunts" and popular ways. The Hanover hunter was none other than Patrick Henry and he wore buckskin breeches and a coonskin cap like his new found neighbors. Louisa, next to Augusta, was the greatest county in Virginia, and it was filled with the cabins of a teeming population of farmers and small proprietors who had escaped the hard conditions of the ridges and sandy plains of the old counties between the James and York and the York and Rappahannock rivers. Orange, Rappahannock and Augusta counties made up the West, the first "land of opportunity" for the restless people of the "Tidewater." And this west extended from a little above the present Richmond to the sites of Cincinnati and Pittsburg—a princely domain which in young Jefferson's day was filled with game and Indians and the fathers of the men who planned the Revolution and largely fought its battles. Not only the Jeffersons, but the Madisons, Monroes, Marshalls and Lewises dwelt in this region, and here Washington surveyed Fairfax lands and later found recruits for his army when all other sections failed him.

With a thorough training in the rudiments of Latin and Greek and an even more thorough knowledge of the strong men of the backwoods, young Jefferson was next sent, at the age of seventeen, to the College of William and Mary, then the best seat of learning in America. He was very tall, very awkward, timid by nature, uncomfortable in the presence of greatness and exceedingly homely. He had the distinction of being the homeliest youth in school—his eyes were gray-blue and restless, his cheek bones were high and his thin freckled skin covered no superfluous flesh, while his hands and feet were large and bony.

Naturally gifted and always ready to learn, he studied his environment, "sized up" his companions and professors and within a short time was gaining more from the new environment, it is safe to say, than any other youth in school. Aristocratic Virginia centered in and around Williamsburg. In the town were the winter houses of the great planters who came in to attend the sessions of His Majesty's royal council when the burgesses assembled which, like the House of Commons in England, generally met the last week of November. The great wigs of Virginia drove into Williamsburg in their stately but creaking family carriages preceded by outriders, front and rear, to scare off the pigs and cattle that roamed at will about the village common or to warn presumptuous people against encroaching too close upon eighteenth century dignity. The great lords of Virginia when young Jefferson was a student at William and Mary were the Braxtons, Lees, Randolphs and Carters, all devoted to the good English ways of Walpole's day, fox-hunters, deep drinkers, ceremonious and formal gentlemen who loved office and office-holding like the Duke of Newcastle, their exemplar. To be a member of the council gave a Virginian the relative rank and standing of a "noble lord" in England and the great families strove, intrigued and bribed to secure the coveted position. An important cause of Richard Henry Lee's entering upon the revolutionary career was his failure to receive this honor, though one of his brothers was in the council. William Beverly of Essex offered £200 for the office of Secretary to the council for which John Carter had paid 1500 guineas in hard cash. Plantation masters strove for new plantations and bought negroes and patented new lands and lavishly entertained the governors both in their Williamsburg houses and on their country estates in order that they and their descendants might be rated as "first families." The greatest honor open to a Virginian was membership in the council; Washington himself recognized this and strove manfully to attain it. While too much stress must not be put upon social life and mere honors, it is true that the love of these distinctions and the desire to lead in Colonial Virginia were mainsprings of the law of entails and negro slavery—privilege then, as now, was the high road to social eminence.

The son of Peter Jefferson from the backwoods was also the son of a Randolph and despite the boy's uncouth looks and awkward ways he was welcomed to the homes of the great, where no doubt his real abilities found expression. He "played the fiddle," danced and could turn a deft hand at cards; he "fell in love" with Judy Burwell or "Sukey" Potter which was no drawback to a young man of parts, but he had no notion of marrying—young Jefferson was too well-balanced, too discreet to make a premature alliance, even with the daughter of so great a house as that of the Burwells of the Pamunky valley in Hanover. He was at home at the gay and rollicksome house of Governor Botetourt whom the burgesses loved well enough to honor with the name of one of the great back-country counties whose limits embraced all Kentucky. But young Jefferson enjoyed most perhaps the free fun of a holiday visit to Hanover where he saw the true burgess stock —the Lyons, Symes, Winstons and even Patrick Henry, then a sort of renegade son of a poor country gentleman.

The orphan boy from Albemarle was more, however, than a mere pleasure seeker—he stood at "the top of his classes" and enjoyed in consequence the companionship of some of his teachers, especially that of Professor Small the mathematician and naturalist whom Jefferson pronounced then and afterward the foremost scientist of America. From 1760 to 1767 the young man remained a student at William and Mary and in the latter year, having gained both the academic honors of graduation and his license to practise law, he returned to Albemarle to take up the serious business of life—serious indeed as it proved to be. He was like many other young Virginians of the time—John Taylor and James Madison, his juniors to be sure,—a real scholar. Latin, Greek and French he knew well enough to retain and enjoy all his life; in law, history and jurisprudence he was quite as well versed as the best men of the country; and in manners he had drunk from the Chesterfield fountain from which Botetourt and his set so frequently drew, and which was to serve the future party leader and president to such good purpose. But while he saw all sides of life as lived at Williamsburg and learned from all, he was not a part of that gay, social and frivolous group which viewed "all the world as a stage and all men as mere actors upon it"; he was at heart a western man with eastern polish, with a touch, too, of the sentimentalism which, somehow, reached him from the then great capital of thought and philosophy—Paris, but without the least stain of the immorality which, in the forms of license and drunkenness, was so common in the "best society" of the Old Dominion. It was indeed a very good education which Jefferson received at the little provincial college and at the cost of less than two pounds, Virginia currency, a month!

When Jefferson "hung out his shingle" in Albemarle he was a little more than twenty-four years old. His practice became immediately lucrative, averaging £3000 a year until the great work of the Revolution called him to other tasks. His friend, Henry, was at that time winning a similar income in Hanover. It is rather a suggestive commentary on the character of Virginia life just before the Revolution to find two young men like these both rather out of the main current of colonial activity "making fortunes" at the law. Wythe and Pendleton were the great lawyers who received twice as much from their clients; and one must remember five thousand a year in Virginia in 1772 was the equivalent of twenty thousand of our money. But Virginia was a great country at that time and there was much "lawing" about entails and "negro property" and land titles. The hill counties of Louisa and Amherst and Pittsylvania were teeming with a restless population and most gentlemen of the older lowland counties had patents to great tracts of land in Watauga, Kentucky or Augusta, names which in Jefferson's day suggested the great areas which we know respectively as Tennessee, Kentucky and West Virginia, and the lawyers had much to do to "keep things straight" or perhaps to tangle matters so that another generation of lawyers would be needed to clear them up.

Five years after Jefferson left William and Mary and when his estate had increased from 1900 acres of land to 5000 and his negroes from thirty to fifty in number, he married Mrs. Skelton, widow of a prominent lowlander and daughter of a wealthy planter and lawyer of James City county. The dowry of the wife was equal to the husband's entire estate and the Virginian of that day may have looked upon the young man from the upper Rivanna as a "captain of industry," dangerous almost to the security of the state. From law $3000 a year and from the plantation

$2000, not to speak of the increase of the negroes! And then to marry a wife whose property was quite as great as his. An income of $9000 or $10,000 a year, or $25,000 of our money. Jefferson was in fact an important man in Virginia when he began his beautiful house on Monticello at the outbreak of the Revolution. While Jefferson was an eminent lawyer in 1774 and his income from his profession was steadily increasing, he was not a real lawyer; he did not love the law nor even respect it as a calling. His real vocation was that of a farmer, relatively small as was the income from that source. His deliberate opinion was: "Those who labor in the earth are the chosen people of God, if ever he had a chosen people; whose breasts he has made his peculiar deposit for substantial and genuine virtue." And if Jefferson was disqualified for law as a calling he was still less fitted for politics—the one thing which the world associates with his name.

II

But men's lives are not their own, "rough hew them as they may." Jefferson was not to be merely an Albemarle planter and master, shipping his tobacco and corn down the Rivanna each autumn and receiving from his Richmond factor his annual draft on some stable English or northern bank. This young man already preeminent for his wealth, devoted to his farm and his plain farmer neighbors, was just the man to send down to Williamsburg in 1773 to help the burgesses properly resist the encroachments of the mother country upon the interests of the colonies. Already Jefferson had seen a little of public life; he had been sent on the same mission to the capital in 1769 but the legislature was dismissed by his quondam friend, the Governor, in such short order that the young member from Albemarle hardly had time to draft a set of resolutions, though he had joined the recalcitrant members in the Raleigh tavern and there signed the famous non-importation agreement which was to give the British ministry no end of trouble.

But in 1773 the mature Jefferson was in Williamsburg; then his great career began and he was never again to be either lawyer or farmer but statesman. In order to get into the drift of things in Virginia at the outbreak of the Revolution it is necessary to review briefly the work of Patrick Henry. That then famous man had begun his career in Hanover by embracing the cause of the Presbyterian preachers and missionaries who were dealing the established church and ministry such sturdy blows that many wise heads were wondering what to do with the arrant dissenters. A little later another pest was added: the Baptists, singing, praying and weeping, invaded conservative, respectable "Tidewater" and to these were added the Methodists in 1772 who threatened to capture all the southside counties.[1] Rousing themselves to the danger of their situation the clergy and the vestries of the Establishment undertook now to defend themselves. The dissenting preachers were declared to be disturbers of the peace and thrust into noisome prisons in a dozen counties. But the people flocked to the prison doors to hear the "good tidings." A revolution was already on and there was no stopping it. What Henry had done was first to arouse the

[1] "Southside" in Virginia refers to the large strip of country south of the James river and east of the Blue Ridge mountains.

THOMAS JEFFERSON

anger of the people against the established church and then to turn the tide of discontent and resentment from the old church toward the cumbersome reactionary system of government which the English ministry had long toyed with in America. Henry was also a "populist."

When he first aspired to a seat in the House of Burgesses, his aristocratic neighbors in Hanover swore that such a man should never disgrace their old county, that he could never be elected from Hanover. Henry, who was already a western man in spirit moved to Louisa, the backwoods county just west of Hanover where young Jefferson had but recently learned his Greek and Latin forms. Henry had worn buckskin breeches as a hunter; he now put them on as a politician. He knew the language of the backwoods already; he now made it his own and never afterward spoke correctly the vernacular of the privileged, of the Hanover gentry who preferred his exile to the disgrace of his elevation in their community: Henry became a burgess from the western county and a leader of the whole up-country, the "Qo'hees," against the compact "Tidewater," the "Tuckahoes." It was the West against the East, the dissenter in religion against the established and formal church.

What followed the advent of Henry in Virginia politics was the mobilization of the middle classes in the whole colony as well as the sturdy backwoodsmen. There were thirty-five counties on the lower reaches of the Virginia rivers, bays and inlets and twenty-nine among the hills and mountains. But not all the thirty-five were in the hands of the plantation lords, who never made up a twentieth of the Virginia people, though a majority of all the counties were probably on the side of the King and Church in 1765; and it had not been difficult for John Robinson, the Speaker of the House, to control legislation in the interest of the East and of the old order and to suppress most popular movements from the West. But the hold of the East upon the community was broken by an alliance which Henry made with Richard Henry Lee who represented a discontented element of the old order. Richard Henry Lee was very able and very ambitious. He had been disappointed in his campaign of 1762 for a place

THOMAS JEFFERSON

in the council and again for the appointment as stamp collector in 1764; moreover Washington of the Northern Neck had been preferred in 1755 as the leader of the Virginia forces in the Braddock campaign while Lee, a representative of a greater house, had been openly snubbed by Governor Dinwiddie and General Braddock. Lee had not been in a good humor these ten years past. In 1763 he began an investigation into the conduct of Speaker Robinson who was at the same time Treasurer of the colony. The investigation dragged on two or three years. Henry supported Lee; the up-country was married to the insurgent element of the East. The result was that Robinson was shown to have been a lender of the public funds, to the extent of £103,000 proclamation money, without security. Not only so; the money had been loaned to needy politicians who were members of the burgesses and who had always "stood by" the machine. Robinson had long been dictator in the House and he, not the "free burgesses," had made the laws. Up-country men now saw why it had been impossible to get new counties created in their region, why the East had been so indifferent to protecting the western country against the Indians; and the middle class population who composed the majority even in the Tidewater counties sympathized with the West, and, now that their old machine was shown to have been honeycombed with corruption, they joined the standards of Henry and Lee. The Speaker was manfully supported by the "people of quality," the Braxtons and Corbins and even by Pendleton, a fair-minded man but always a stickler for the forms of law. Robinson died under a cloud and his partisans did not rally again until the close of the Revolution. His property was seized in part by the Colony, but the bulk of the great embezzlement was never repaid.

When Jefferson was a college boy he was in sympathy with the new West and was a friend of Henry though a younger man by ten years. The party which Henry and Lee had created and which was still in power when the great quarrel with England came to a crisis was composed of the people of the twenty-one counties of Virginia which covered the area now known as the

Piedmont and extended to the Redstone settlements on the Monongahela and the Ohio in the northwest and to the Watauga settlements in the southwest. Small farmers along the upper rivers, tobacco growers from the ridges between, hunters and trappers from the slopes of the Alleghanies and the hitherto inert and unorganized mass of small proprietors and slave-owners from the old counties, made up the rank and file of the party—a party with which the great majority of the people sympathized and acted for ten years after 1769. The leaders were first of all Henry, then Richard Henry Lee and George Mason, both aristocrats but patriots at the same time. Washington, notwithstanding his relations with Lee, gradually came over, though many of his friends had been, and some still remained, connected with the men who had formerly ruled Virginia. Between 1769 and 1779 Henry and Lee with their powerful following ruled the burgesses or the legislature as completely as had Robinson and his group.

Jefferson had grown up in this party; he was close to Henry; his county and neighboring counties worshiped the great orator who had made Virginia famous for eloquence; and his younger friends Dabney Carr and "Jimmie" Madison were of the same mind. As a lieutenant of Henry the young scholar from Albemarle entered politics in 1774 and he was a follower of no mean sort, a student, a keen lawyer, a good writer and popular with the common people. Many long years the minority had struggled for a hearing; the western counties had gradually grown to be the most populous; they had filled up with Scotch-Irish from Pennsylvania and Germans from the Palatinate most of whom were serious minded men who built log churches on the frontier, established schools, like Liberty Academy, in the wilderness, and sent to Princeton for their preachers and teachers. They believed in God as creator of the universe, a future state of rewards and punishments and the mystery of the Trinity, and if they got a chance, like the Puritans of New England, they would put these ideas into their organic law,[1]

[1] Witness the first constitution of Tennessee, also that of North Carolina.

THOMAS JEFFERSON

or compel their opponents to accept their creed. Their eastern allies were largely Baptists who knew what persecution for conscience sake was and who, if their voice could be heard, would make religious freedom a part of the constitution. Verily these were not the men who had made Virginia in the past; they were the men, though, who were to make the Virginia of 1800.

Still the people who looked to Princeton as a source of all religious orthodoxy and found their cultural ideas in the neighborhood of Philadelphia could never have made Virginia great. Neither could the numerous but illiterate Baptists with their simple-minded pastors have erected the great social fabric which the world came to know as Virginia. It required leadership, knowledge of the world, philosophy; and these elements Jefferson and his group, Madison, John Taylor and Spencer Roane, all trained in the best schools of the time, students and philosophers by nature, supplied. These younger men, like Henry, only infinitely better grounded in the learning of the world, were admirers of the insurgent Whigs of England, the fallen Earl of Chatham, the great orator Burke and his rival the brilliant Fox. The ideals of the best elements of the Whig party in England were grafted upon the rough honesty and unyielding purpose of the Virginia up-country. Such was the party which held the upper hand in Virginia when Massachusetts cried aloud for help in 1774 and it need not be added the cry fell not upon deaf ears. The young party was cousin-german to New England. Princeton and Yale were close akin and the religious ideals of Massachusetts were only another brand of the stern Calvinism which dominated the rank and file of Virginia.

But Jefferson was no Calvinist, even if Henry was; and Madison was a member of the established church. However, both Jefferson and Madison believed in the new doctrine of popular rule. What the majority wished was law to them; they believed in the people as New Englanders did not. And the first article of Henry's creed was majority rule—a majority of all the people who had a share in the commonwealth. Recent history in Virginia compelled this and Whig teaching in England tended the same way.

It is not difficult then to see how the great principle of Jefferson's life—absolute faith in democracy—came to him. He was the product of the first West in American history; he grew up with men who ruled their country well, who fought the Indians valiantly, who made of a vast wilderness a smiling garden and most of whose ills were due to the former absence of self government in the larger affairs of Virginia life. Jefferson loved his backwoods neighbors and he in turn was loved by them. There was perfect sympathy. "The man who follows the daily round of agriculture is God's noblest handiwork."

The events of 1774 and 1775 made the Virginia leaders world figures and Jefferson, not Henry, was soon to become the author of the Declaration of Independence, the champion before mankind of the oppressed. Henry essayed the national rôle in 1774; but he was clearly the man to lead the party at home, not in the greater arena. Lee was in the congress of 1776 and as the oldest and most aristocratic member of the delegation, he introduced the resolution for independence and logically he should have headed the committee which drafted the famous Declaration. But the old feud with the Washingtons was not yet quieted. It would have been a great risk to allow Lee too much prominence and the plan to substitute Jefferson was proposed and Lee found it necessary to hasten off to Virginia to "mend his political fences." Jefferson, Henry and Washington were on good terms. Washington's friends and, what was more important, the large group of old families still smarting under the chastisement which Lee had given them in 1765-66 were spared the humiliation of seeing the renegade Lee a national hero. Devious are the ways of high politics.

Notwithstanding the intrigue and wire-pulling which was employed to retire Lee at that time, Jefferson was entirely worthy of the honor which came to him—he was indeed the man of all Virginians to become the spokesman of America; the language of the Declaration was the language of dissent and complaint which had been heard in Virginia for a quarter of a century, and Jefferson could well lead a fight against the same kind of privilege and arbitrary power as applied to all America which he and his neighbors had overthrown in Virginia. The cause of the West in Virginia was the cause of America before the world.

But the forces which Henry and Lee had overthrown were not to be put aside at a single brush of the political besom. Henry was not the master in Virginia, though the most powerful single individual. Even with his co-workers, Mason and Lee, he still fell short of the power which certain present-day "bosses" exercise, as was clearly shown in 1775 when, raising his regiment of Hanover and Louisa militia, he seized the powder which Governor Dunmore was about to employ against the revolutionists. All eyes were upon the zealous self-made colonel and so popular was the up-country leader that it was impossible to prevent the convention then in session from making him general of the Virginia troops. That Henry was a good military chieftain may well be doubted; but his old time enemies were determined he should have no chance to prove this point. Henry's brother-in-law, William Campbell, with no military training except what the backwoods afforded, won the battle of Kings Mountain in 1780 and his friend, George Rogers Clark, manifested all the qualities of a good general in his famous campaign in the Northwest in 1779. When Henry was placed in command by the convention of the new state a committee of safety was appointed by the same delegates of the people, a majority of whom were Henry's enemies and some of whom had been connected with the Robinson scandal; Edmund Pendleton was its chairman. The committee of safety had general oversight of the defenses of Virginia in the summer and autumn of 1775 when Sir Henry Clinton and Sir Peter Parker planned and sought to execute the first great scheme for the conquest of the South. Things were so managed by Pendleton and his committee that ardent and popular Henry never heard a gunshot, while a subordinate, Colonel Woodford, was put into practical command of the troops which were nominally subject only to Henry's orders! Woodford won the first victory in the South at Great Bridge near Norfolk on December 9, 1775, while Henry was compelled to lie idle at Williamsburg. There was not to be any "General

Henry" in Virginia though "Mr. Henry" might still count for much.

This was the first setback to Henry's forward and vigorous program; Lee's humiliation came a little later. The men, like Edmund Pendleton, who managed both schemes, thoroughly enjoyed their brief success. It began to look as if the "interests" of the old days would govern revolutionary Virginia. The reply of the up-country party to this treatment of their hero was his election by the next convention to the governorship of the state, to the position just vacated by His Majesty's royal representative, Lord Dunmore—a very high honor and next to Washington's the most important position in America in 1776. The reactionaries had played their game too well.

But the great work of 1776 in Virginia was the framing of the fundamental law of the new state —the constitution which was to be the model for the next seventy-five years in most southern and western communities, faulty as it turned out to be in the important matter of representation. Henry and Lee and Mason were agreed that all the old bulwarks of the English commons should be re-erected in Virginia—and among them the noble Bill of Rights was created, and was made law by the convention, Henry being responsible for the clauses bearing upon religious liberty and Mason for the older ideas of freedom of speech, press and the right of revolution. The constitution of Virginia of 1776 was wonderfully like the program of the English revolution of 1688 and many passages of the Bill of Rights were copied verbatim from Locke's *Essay on Government*. There was nothing original in all the talk about "trial by jury," the "right of revolution" and of "redress of grievances." The older leaders like Pendleton and the reactionaries from the coast counties could listen to agitation of that sort as well as any. What aroused the ire of the beneficiaries of the system of entail and primogeniture, of slavery and great estates, was the demand for proportional representation on the part of the up-country. For a hundred years the small group of eastern planters had denied fair representation to the people on the border, the people who fought the Indians, cleared the lands and made Virginia prosperous. In 1776 they had a majority of the voters, of the actual landowners; their counties were large, however, and entitled only to the same number of delegates to the Assembly as the small Tidewater counties. They had never been able to bring the East to an agreement about the size of the county. What they wanted was a greater vote in the law-making body—a vote commensurate with their numerical and fighting strength; but in 1776 they had only twenty-nine counties as against the thirty-five of the East and whenever a new western county was created a new eastern must also be created regardless of the meager population of the latter.

Jefferson, not in the convention, but a member of the congress at Philadelphia and just now writing the famous Declaration, was one of the leaders in Virginia who held "radical" views on the subjects of suffrage and representation. He believed in manhood suffrage and proportional representation of all the voters and he took the risk of sending to Williamsburg a draft of a constitution embodying his views.[1] This proposed con-

[1] *Works of Thomas Jefferson*, (Ford's Fed. Ed.) II, 158.-183.

stitution would have destroyed forever the power of the privileged planters. Representation in the House was to be in proportion to population and the representatives were to elect the members of the Senate. The House was also to elect the Governor. With the Executive and the Senate dependent upon representatives elected annually by the people, and with the inequalities of the old system of county representation "done away" there would have been little chance for the old régime ever again to control affairs in Virginia—slavery, entails and primogeniture would all have gone together in a few short years and none foresaw this more clearly than Jefferson, the great slave-master.

Not even Henry could stand for so much democracy as this; Lee could not be expected to admire the man who was about to harvest the fame which was properly his; and Mason was content to urge his English ideas of trial by jury, right of revolution and habeas corpus. The old party, the "Tuckahoes" of 1766, rallied their whole strength against any such plan as this which to them would have meant the utter ruin of all "vested interests," the subjugation of "gentlemen of family" to the "ruffians of the West." Jefferson's democratic ideas received scant courtesy from even a revolutionary convention which was itself indirectly an up-country product. The outcome was a constitution which left the power of the new state in the hands of the East and the opponents of all that Henry and Jefferson stood for; there was some juggling of representation, a district system which appeared to make substantial concession to the just demands of the West; but when, a year or two later, the revolutionary ardor was somewhat abated, it was found that the new system simply perpetuated the old—the East in the name of "property" had the majority of delegates in both houses and since the executive was chosen by the legislature in joint session the governor was invariably friendly to the East.

There was much talk of recalling Jefferson from his place in Philadelphia[1] and in fact the vote he received was so small that he, the leader of the Virginia delegation, resigned rather than come in "next to the lag." He had not yet reaped the harvest of fame which was to come from his

[1] *Works of Thomas Jefferson*, II, 198.

authorship of the Declaration and his enemies had thus chosen their only chance to humiliate him.

The time had come for the quiet planter of Albemarle to make his own program and to fight for it while the populous West was at his back and when his fame was still on the increase. He prepared himself and in the summer of 1776 he stood for election to the House of Representatives in Albemarle. It was now unnecessary for him to stand all day at the polls and bow politely to each man who voted for him and to regale all who were thirsty with copious draughts from his "huge bowl of punch." There was no opposition in Albemarle and a half dozen other counties in the up-country would gladly have honored him with their votes.

III

Once in the legislature he began quietly his policy of tearing up the "interests" root and branch. Only a half year before the conservatives and the reactionaries had combined to humiliate him; it would have been more than human in him not to enjoy seeing his opponents

THOMAS JEFFERSON

writhe and wriggle as he marshalled the necessary majorities for his plan, first to do away with entails, second to make unlawful the long practice of primogeniture, or the bestowal upon the oldest son of the landed estates of deceased property owners; the hoary shelter of the privileged order in Virginia, the established church, was next attacked and partially overthrown; the fourth item on his list of reforms, brought down from the up-country, was the gradual abolition of slavery—having succeeded in most of what he had presented, he hoped to carry this too and by the votes of slaveholders like himself! But to bring the great lowland planters to "split" on this question, as they had done on the others, and to allow the very basis of their fabric to be undermined was too much. Slavery remained to curse America for a hundred years yet. Finally he proposed a system of public free schools—still another item in the western economy—for Virginia, which was to be headed by William and Mary College as a state university. In this he scarcely hoped to succeed and of course he failed.

One naturally inquires how such a thorough-going reform could be accomplished or set in motion at a single session of the legislature. Virginia was still filled with the enthusiastic idealism which swept most of the people off their feet, an idealism which seized upon practical and conservative men like Washington as well as upon "dreamers" of the type of Jefferson. It was a time not unlike the famous Fifth of August, 1789, in France, which brought still greater reforms for that country. Henry had been preparing the way for ten years; the up-country leaders and the low-country dissenters had voted and prayed for the same kind of thing since the close of the "old French" war; and the great glittering Declaration, now resounding around the world, had put on the finishing stroke. It was the only time such work could be done and Jefferson was the one man to lead. Rare indeed have been the parallels to these reforms in the history of the world.

Short sighted indeed was the policy of humiliating the radical author of a real constitution in 1776, and perhaps Edmund Pendleton and Wilson C. Nicholas meditated remorsefully on their foolish work of putting this young man out of congress only to have him come down from the hills to the Assembly and demolish them—with his sledge hammer blows!

There were now two stars in the Virginia firmament and both were representatives of the up-country. Could Governor Henry and the author of the Declaration of Independence continue to live peaceably in Virginia and lead the same party? Possibly, but not likely.

Already the great governor and popular tribune was embarrassed and two years later when Jefferson became governor the friends of the older man were careful to put stumbling blocks in the way of the popular young executive and from this time to the end of their lives the two were not friends. Jefferson thought Henry an unlearned and merely rhetorical orator while Henry regarded Jefferson as a dangerous innovator and "infidel". But one or the other must rule the party and Henry was undoubtedly the better man for that.

From the introduction of Jefferson's radical program in 1776 Henry was drawn somewhat from the strong position of former years. He did nothing to aid Jefferson's school system; though he never defended slavery, he was unwilling to risk his popularity in an effort to destroy it; and he actually opposed Jefferson's scheme of disestablishing the Church, although he had won his fame in fighting the Church. It was clear to wiser heads that Henry and Jefferson did not agree and that of the two the latter was the real reformer. Had these two men been able to work together in the momentous revolutionary epoch how different might have been the course of American history!

Henry now settled in the West and for a time he contemplated emigrating to Kentucky—Jefferson who succeeded to the office of governor in 1779 proved half-a-failure as an administrator and Henry's friends were not above demanding an investigation which it was expected would ruin him as a public man. The publicity which was heaped upon the failure of Jefferson to protect Virginia from invasion in 1781 almost destroyed the popularity of the retiring governor. In 1783 he was put "out in the cold," i. e. he was sent

THOMAS JEFFERSON 37

to the already discredited congress of the Confederation. This had been the scene of his greatest success and he was not averse to taking up with his young and devoted friend, Madison, the cause of the nascent nation. He accepted the call which he knew was intended as a sort of balm to his wounded feelings—an easy "letdown" for a man who had been a victim of the circumstances of the late Revolution. Little did he or his enemies think that he would ever again be able to strike such heavy blows as he had struck in 1776 and 1777.

In congress, however, he fought so well the cause of Virginia in her struggle with the northern states to retain her vast western possessions that even Henry warmed toward him again. Jefferson's learning, his talent at arranging differences, of appearing to yield without really yielding, were indispensable to Virginia at this stage of her history. It was Jefferson whose practical turn of mind invented our system of coinage units and saved us from the cumbersome method of the English or of the humorous scheme proposed by Robert Morris. He worked out with Madison the final plan upon which Virginia ceded her western lands to congress and he was the one who first and last insisted that slavery should never be permitted to gain a foothold north of the Ohio. Notable indeed were the services of the banished politician. And finally when the peace came and the treaties were all ratified, congress asked Jefferson to go to France to succeed there the famous Franklin who was returning home to die.

However, Henry was again the great man in the state; he absolutely ruled the legislature; and he was made governor a second time in 1784. Mason and Lee came again to the front and this time as before Henry made a popular executive. He fought now for a protective tariff against "insidious English commerce" and on behalf of the "infant industries" which he hoped to see spring up in the new empire. A great figure was Henry now as ever—jealous of Virginia's fame, popular in manner and as great an orator as when he began his career of revolution twenty years before. No man could stand in the Old Dominion without his actual or supposed friendship. Washington who never loved Henry made

THOMAS JEFFERSON

overtures to him on behalf of his great plan for a national convention; Madison who had never been a close follower sought his support and acknowledged his supremacy. Jefferson could not well sacrifice his self-respect and forget or forgive the events of 1781; but he knew who it was that had succeeded to twice the power in Virginia which George III had surrendered. There has seldom been a more perfect political machine in an American state than that which Henry, during his second term as governor, had at his beck and call.

It is not surprising then that Jefferson accepted from congress in 1784 the mission to France— a post of great honor, from the national point of view, but one which the really big men of Virginia, Henry, Mason and perhaps even Lee, would have declined. Thus Jefferson was to get the very training which he needed and in the service of the nation. Indeed his great work had been and was to continue in the cause of the country, not of Virginia.

Some have said that Jefferson's later attitude toward the federal government was due to his absence from the country during the critical period of 1784-1789. There may be reason in this but I am disposed to think that his later views were only an outgrowth of his earlier experience, a product as well of the highly complicated political situation of Virginia at the time.

Of the long term in France, of his unique record as a minister, or of his influence in the early stages of the "great" Revolution, there is no need to speak. Jefferson returned to America about the time the rejuvenated federal government with Washington at its head went into operation.

During Jefferson's absence in Europe Virginia grew in wealth and power as did no other American commonwealth. Her trade with Europe was flourishing, her teeming population had spread far into the west, Kentucky was a new state of itself but loyal to the Old Dominion, the Redstone settlements counted near a hundred thousand souls, and the Watauga country, the quondam state of Franklin, was half a child of Virginia. And this great domain of lowland, rugged mountain and bounding prairie—more than a hundred thousand square miles—was still the land of Patrick Henry whom the people credited with having brought on the struggle for freedom and with having done most after the war was over for the rights of the common men. He had compelled the nationalists to amend their constitution to suit the popular demand, he had saved to the West the free navigation of the Mississippi. Henry became now an intense particularist and he turned his great party, mainly up-country and western men, overwhelmingly against the growing necessity for a real national power. The westerners and up-country men had formerly been nationalists in tendency, but the threatened loss of the navigation of the Mississippi and the weakness of congress had turned them to Virginia as the only power to protect their rights if it came to actual warfare.

The years 1784 to 1788 brought a revolution in Virginia public sentiment: the real revolutionists, the men who had fought the battles of the war just ended, were now particularists, zealous for a growing and mighty Virginia; while the former conservatives who had always opposed the new counties, who had fought Henry in 1775 and Jefferson in 1776, were now under the leadership of Washington and Jefferson's young friend, Madison, to become the Federalist party. In other words the men who had fought the radicals in 1776 and who ridiculed the Declaration of Independence now became the champions of nationality with the idea of defending themselves against the democracy of the border. Gentlemen who controlled their state as never before, and they counties of eastern Virginia, the rotten boroughs of that day, had counted their strength and, with Washington on their side, believed they could win against their foes. And when the great fight on the adoption of the federal constitution came in 1788 the "property" of the East proved victorious. Eastern men who owned slaves now controlled their state as never before and they were likely to control the new national administration. The federal constitution actually guaranteed them in their ownership of slaves and gave them increased representation in congress because of their "peculiar property."

Jefferson came back to Virginia more radical

as to personal rights than when he went away and to him the necessity of breaking down all class distinctions was imperative. What position would he take in Virginia politics? To join Henry and his own former followers would have been repudiation of much of his own past work and of his closest friend, Madison; to join Washington meant alliance with the men who had tried to destroy him and all his program in 1776. He was at heart a nationalist, but a leveler. He joined Washington and accepted a post in the cabinet but tried to escape the alliance with the ancient "Tuckahoes." The result was that he, with all his address as a compromiser, gained few friends among the conservatives and none with the Henry party. Madison was close to him, but Grayson, Monroe and Richard Henry Lee must have doubted either his loyalty to Virginia or his honesty as a leader. The "old war horse" from Red Hill held him in contempt.

But Jefferson was not reduced to the necessity of making an issue in order to escape the dilemma. Hamilton and the extreme conservatives now put forward their policy looking toward increasing the powers and functions of the federal government beyond even the implications of the constitution. In 1790 the foreign obligations of the former confederacy, amounting to nearly $8,000,000, were funded at par. To this no objection was made. Next it was proposed to issue government bonds to all holders of domestic obligations, estimated at $44,414,085, which had been bandied about at a fourth or even a tenth of their face value and most of which obligations had been bought up by speculators who were now urging upon congress the adoption of the new policy. Finally it was a part of Hamilton's scheme to have the national government take over $18,000,000 of the state debts contracted during the Revolution. Virginia made no opposition to the arrangement of the foreign debt; but to the assumption at par of the millions of claims against the confederation for which the holders in 1790 had paid only a small fraction of the face value, most leaders of opinion in that state made strenuous objection. Madison voiced a well-nigh universal feeling when he spoke long and ardently against this part of the program of his former friend. When, however, the state debt proposition came up not only Virginia but all the South, except South Carolina, revolted, for the southern states, especially Virginia, owed very little. It was not difficult for the plainest man to see that for the nation to assume a debt of $18,000,000, two thirds of which was owed by the northern states, and then tax all alike for its payment was unjust.

This was not all. At the last session of the First Congress Hamilton succeeded in establishing a national bank to which Virginians were also universally opposed. The whole scheme was completed when at the same session in 1791 a federal excise tax of twenty-five cents a gallon should be laid upon all whiskey manufactured in the country. This was a particularly burdensome tax to the backwoods men, as they were accustomed to distil their grain and then transport it to eastern markets. And Virginia was largely a back-country state. What was especially irritating to Virginia members of congress during all the debates on these bills was Hamilton's undisguised purpose to increase the powers of the national government at the expense of the states. The assumption bill, the bank and the excise schemes had, all, this avowed purpose. To add to the weight of unpopularity of the new government Washington and Hamilton and John Adams assumed an importance and established a ceremonial which the farmers of Virginia resented. Henry declared on one occasion that he could not accept office under the federal government because he would not be able at his time of life to adapt himself to the regal manners of the new régime.

Madison who had always been hostile to Henry and friendly to Hamilton broke with the Federalists. Jefferson who had been less of a nationalist joined his young friend, and the two began the organization in 1792 of the party which was soon to embrace all the small farmers of the South and which eight years later won control of the federal power which Hamilton had been so industriously augmenting. And from 1792 to 1796 the leaders of the new party held up to ridicule most of the acts of the Washington administration and made great capital out of the birthday parties and other innocent social doings of the President and his family.

This, it would seem, would have been the occasion for Henry to take courage and put himself at the head of the party of resistance in Virginia and dispute with Jefferson its leadership in the country. Nothing of the sort happened. As soon as Jefferson began his opposition to the national government and to appeal to the great mass of country people in Virginia, the "old war horse" of earlier days began to seek out occasions to express his approval of Washington, "the great and good man," from whom he had demanded an explanation of his course in 1788. It was not a long while before the greatest of all anti-federalists was known in Philadelphia to be a convert! And forthwith Washington offered the former antagonist the highest office at his command. The outcome was that Henry became the most enthusiastic of Virginia Federalists and canvassed for a seat in the legislature at Washington's request simply that he might there oppose Jefferson and his friends, Madison and John Taylor, in their efforts to have the alien and sedition laws repealed. Henry had yielded somewhat of his principles in 1776 when he supported a constitution which sacrificed his followers, the small farmers; but he had regained his immense popularity in the struggle of 1786-1788.

Now he lost his following and the young upstart, John Randolph, was listened to at Charlotte Courthouse, in April 1798, as he ridiculed the old statesman. Jefferson won the place which his older rival had surrendered and Madison was next in succession. Having retired from the Washington administration at the beginning of 1794, Jefferson devoted himself for the next six years to building up and consolidating all the forces of opposition. Everywhere he was regarded as the leader of the radical forces in the community. A philosopher who had been counted among the famous men of France during his residence there, a politician who resigned the first position in the cabinet because he was too democratic for that environment, a planter and farmer whose house was admittedly the handsomest in America and whose income was popularly estimated at many thousands a year, an inventor of new plows, a writer of books and most of all the author of the great Declaration of Independence which was coming into greater popularity in the South every year—such was the man now inspiring the Virginia democracy and organizing the courthouse cliques after the manner of the revolutionists in 1776.

There was an opposition: Washington exerted himself to the uttermost in 1798 and 1799; Henry was Washington's close second as has been noted; John Marshall spent six thousand dollars to win a seat in Congress in 1798; the Bassetts in lower Hanover and New Kent gave in their support to the conservative forces which were supposed to be fighting for the very existence of organized society, and Henry Lee, the father of the greatest of all the Lees, went about sowing seeds of discord in the hope that the dangerous democrat might be defeated. Smaller men fought in smaller ways but none the less bitterly. Virginia was rent asunder as never before; the hills and the mountains, the people of the great counties of the back-country, followed the standards erected by their neighbor of Monticello;

the towns, the smaller counties of the East, all the appointees of the federal government, the judges of the federal courts, entered the canvass against the "mobocrat," the innovator, the author of the law which had taken away the right of the older sons to the paternal acres.

IV

Though Jefferson dreaded conflict and shrank like a woman from publicity, he continued to lead; he worked out party programs, called councils of his lieutenants and contributed of his means to the party chest. Everywhere and at all times he was the source of inspiration to those who gathered about him or who received his long and thoughtful letters. Defeated in the campaign of 1796 for the presidency he accepted the vice-presidency with the utmost willingness, "having put his hands to the plow." And while he presided over a senate, two thirds of whose members were his political or personal enemies, he never once forgot himself, like Calhoun of later years, or showed signs of partisanship. It was the author of the Declaration of Independence, the former foreign minister and secretary of state who presided over the Senate which actually threatened to impeach him for giving a letter of introduction to his friend Logan who was going to France on a self-imposed mission of peace in 1798. Yet he was the soul of courtesy to Sedgwick of Massachusetts and Tracy of Connecticut, his most malignant foes; and in December, 1799, when all but himself had lost their poise and dignity in their anger or joy at the President for proposing the famous peace commission to France, he could quietly call the Senate to order. Secure in the growing affections of the masses of people, he could view the rebuffs which were meted out to him in Philadelphia by the rabble stirred up by his opponents, or endure with the utmost equanimity the nightly shrieks and cat calls of hostile serenaders beneath his windows, knowing full well that his day was dawning. Few men have been reviled as was Jefferson during the closing years of the eighteenth century. In Virginia a pious matron of a noted family wished that he might never have a son to succeed him, and in Massachusetts men prayed daily that the atheist, and arch-enemy of all good men and noble causes, might be brought to justice for his scandalous blasphemy. Never faltering, growing more simple in his democratic ways as he grew more famous, he kept his course—riding about his plantation when in Virginia or meeting his friends Madison, Albert Gallatin of Pennsylvania, Nathaniel Macon of North Carolina, at unostentatious dinners at the "Indian Queen" when at the seat of government. So far did he carry his leveling principles that he could not be induced to take a place at the head of the table where his devoted followers made up the guests, but always chose, like the man in the Bible story, the least prominent station—even after his election to the presidency.

When the conflict was over, when both Henry and Washington had gone to their graves weeping for their country because it followed Jefferson, when his former friend Adams turned from him as from a leper, having, however, placed in the chair of Chief Justice his strongest enemy in Virginia, John Marshall, he had the great mass of the southern people behind him, the majority in Pennsylvania, New York and Vermont and a strong following in Connecticut and Massachusetts. He had drawn a line from northeast to southwest, from the town of Portsmouth in New Hampshire to Augusta in Georgia, west and north of which almost every man was his devoted admirer and east and south of which he had many friends and some leaders of the people. Jefferson had changed the first sectional line separating North from South to one separating the older from the newer sections of all the states and by his policy and his devotion to popular rights this was soon to disappear, leaving only isolated groups of opponents like the Essex neighborhood in Massachusetts or the old river counties of the Carolinas.

What this apostle of democracy had stood for in Virginia, the dogma that all men are free and equal, equality before the law, popular suffrage, equal representation of equal units of population in all legislatures, abolition of negro slavery and the establishment of religious freedom—the creed of the up-country of the South before 1820—was now the national program and Virginia became the basis and the background for the federal administration in the same way that the up-country counties in Virginia had been the basis and support of the Revolution in 1776. Jefferson had captured Henry's party in Virginia, rejuvenated it, found allies for it in the Carolina up-country, and then made it national. And it was this growing section of the South, the populous border region, now spread into Tennessee and Kentucky and Ohio, Presbyterians, Baptists and Methodists, considered in denominational terminology, that contributed the ideals which made Jefferson's first four years in office unparalleled in American history and which caused his policy to prevail even in New England. This it seems to the writer is the key to the understanding of the remarkable popularity of the third president, notwithstanding the almost complete breakdown of his second term in office.

Strange as it may seem, Jefferson was not at one with any great group of his followers: he hated war, yet the up-country people were the most warlike in the nation; he was liberal in religious matters while the Scotch-Irish, Baptist and Methodist masses who made up his party were devoted to Calvinistic theology or to positive acception of the miraculous view of the New Testament; he was in all his tastes and activities a gentleman and a scholar, they were the cruder, the more illiterate great element of the American nationality. What kept them together? What stirred their enthusiasm for the greatest scholar and thinker who has yet occupied the presidential chair?

Jefferson had a boundless faith in the masses. He still adhered to his doctrine that most farmers are honest while most other people are dishonest. God was to him especially intimate with the farmers—"their breasts were still the Almighty's chosen repository of truth." Jefferson thought all men ought to have the ballot—that was his remedy for the ills of his time, though he hastened to add that all men should be educated at public expense. Jefferson hated England and the backcountry people had no less antipathy for the nation which Patrick Henry had held up to them and their fathers as the cause of all America's woes, as the insidious foe who still stirred up the

Indians to deeds of rapine and bloodshed. So if Jefferson did not share the religious zeal and dogmatism of the people who supported him, if he viewed Jesus, the Christ, as a plain but very great teacher and philosopher, he had faith in his followers; he liked their democratic church and ideas of government and their simple every-day honesty. Their methods he undertook to apply to the federal system. Was it not he who said: All men are created free and equal? That was their creed in politics as well as in church affairs. Whether Jefferson believed this glittering doctrine or not, he hated all men who undertook to establish the contrary principle. All such sought, in his opinion, some undue advantage in society, some undue attention and that was contrary to the democracy which he hoped to see prevail in America. Thus one sees easily how sectarians, religious zealots, political doctrinaires and all men who believed in essential human freedom, broken, though they were, into hostile groups, found in Jefferson their common point of union. And the alliance which resulted was a party of practical idealists in this country, never

THOMAS JEFFERSON

likely to reappear—a party of peasant farmers led by a great peasant planter in a nation ninety-five per cent of whom were peasant farmers. No wonder the Jefferson party stood intact for more than a quarter of a century.

Now when this ideal back-country man became president he continued the same democratic manner of life which had prevailed in Albemarle county and all the other counties in the nation. The people rejoiced to hear that "levees had been done away," that the President admitted all who came to see him on equal terms; they were glad to know there were no more state carriages with outriders and footmen and that the President rode about the little backwoods capital on the Potomac in quite as simple a manner as any farmer who carried a bag of corn to mill.

When Jefferson was president he had for his cabinet members his friend and neighbor Madison—a farmer like himself—another personal friend Albert Gallatin, an able leader of the backwoods people of Pennsylvania, who proved in a practical way quite as good a Secretary of Treasury as Hamilton himself had been. Nathaniel

Macon, a typical southern farmer, who lived miles away from any public highway, and whose theory in life was, that, when his neighbors came near enough for him to hear their dogs bark, he would go further west, received Jefferson's support and was elected Speaker of the House. The only great aristocrat in the party, Charles Pinckney, with an annual income of half a hundred thousand, was appropriately made a foreign minister. The ideas of the small farmers, not those of the great planters or merchant princes, dominated the whole administration and strangely enough the "large affairs" of the country seem not to have suffered. There was no proscription of the rival party. Federalists held all the offices and Federalists made no secret of their hatred for the President. They thought themselves the repository of ability and learning and respectability; and all their papers and organs daily published diatribes against the "fools and knaves" who had come to power. But Jefferson was a patient man. He did not remove a baker's dozen of his opponents. Death and resignation came only slowly to his assistance, and some of his followers were office-hungry.

Washington had set the example of appointing only Federalists to office. Every member of the federal courts was both a Federalist and a personal friend of the first president; the district judges, attorneys and marshals were partisans, some of them of the most virulent character. And after retiring from the presidency, Washington insisted that members of the other party should not be appointed even to the positions in the army which he was organizing to fight France in 1798. Adams had not departed from this rule. But Jefferson said we are all Republicans, all Federalists, and his purpose was to unite all moderate men upon the single and simple principle of democracy. And he was almost successful.

The two great measures of Jefferson's eight years in office were the purchase of Louisiana and the Embargo. Many people were surprised that the peacemaker and idealist should have threatened war with France, for whom he was supposed peculiarly to stand in national politics, if he were not given control of the mouth of the

Mississippi. But any one who studied carefully the make-up of the Jefferson party must have seen that it was the free navigation of the Mississippi which the great body of his followers demanded. Three great states, Kentucky, Tennessee and Ohio had been built up by these very followers and the one condition of their economic existence was the free navigation of the great river. The interior counties of all the states from New York to Georgia were all favorable to the demands of the people on the "western waters." Only the commercial interests of the East were indifferent to the matter. Hence it was a foregone conclusion that Jefferson, the "pacifist," should take the stand he did in 1802 and write to the American minister in Paris, that "from the day France takes possession of New Orleans she makes us an enemy, and we must marry ourselves to the British fleet and nation." No politician counts consistency as "worth a straw" when the interests of his party and constituents are thrown into the balance. Jefferson, the arch-enemy of England, was now her friend if by such a summersault he could win for his western friends the coveted prize. The Constitution thus became, even in Jefferson's hands, a very elastic document—"nothing of moment among friends." The man who had moved heaven and earth because Washington and Adams stretched the sacred document of 1787 now tore it to pieces and all his friends of a former day applauded. Only Adams rubbed his eyes. The most popular act of Jefferson's presidency was the purchase of Louisiana which was accomplished a year after he opened the question with France—it made certain the allegiance of the West and the supremacy of the new party.

The next and only great item of Jefferson's policy I mean to discuss here is the famous Embargo of 1807. The warring powers of Europe had decided that there should be no neutrals in the struggle, that America, fast becoming the mistress of the carrying trade of the world, because of her neutrality, must take sides. Jefferson desired to sell freely to all parties, "to make hay while the sun shines." But when England and France pressed hard upon American commerce, trying to compel him to take sides, his answer was, "stop all trade with both parties" and starve them into a recognition of the demands of the United States. And to make sure of his policy he forbade all American shipping to leave port. Millions of dollars worth of goods in ships worth other millions rotted in our harbors, out of reach of hostile hands. This was firing the barn to get rid of the rats. Never did a president attempt to enforce a more unpopular act. Virginia lost enormously, Jefferson himself sacrificing half his annual income; but if Virginia lost half her annual crop values New England lost three fourths. The President was attacked in the eastern papers more savagely than John Adams had ever been in the southern; political speakers held him up as a monster devouring the substance of the land; ministers shouted denunciation from a thousand pulpits; and aspiring poets won laurels by lampooning the President. But the President was a resolute man notwithstanding his sensitiveness to public criticism. He was an idealist and he was right in the assumption that a year or two of absolute non-intercourse with Europe would bring the desired results, recognition of the right to a neutral commerce with all the warring powers of the world; but he was wrong in the premise that men in general, especially American merchants and seamen who had been accustomed for a hundred years to violate with impunity all the laws they did not like, would submit to the necessary restrictions upon their actions. Jefferson was philosopher enough to see that if he lost one crop of tobacco he would get a market for all his future crops and he was willing to wait; the majority of planters in Virginia, being now in the ascendency in national and state affairs, were induced to support their leader, though with many a grimace. But New England was the commercial center—there Jefferson was regarded as an enemy, there men had for three generations "gone down to the sea in ships" whether the law favored or forbade. They felt no great love for law anyway; certainly none for a law which originated in Virginia. They simply defied the President; and Napoleon wittily remarked when he seized many valuable cargoes of New England goods that he was only helping the American government enforce the law.

When the Embargo broke down and the popularity which so warmed the cockles of Jefferson's heart was gone he, like a woman unconvinced, "stood pat." Nothing could move him and he went out of office in March, 1809, amidst the hoots and cries of derision not unlike those to which his ears had been accustomed when Adams was president and he presided over the Senate. Nevertheless, he, unlike Adams, had put his friend in the place he vacated willingly and Madison could placate the angry commercialists. It was not a triumphal procession, his return to Monticello; but when he arrived at Charlottesville his faithful mountain neighbors had assembled to greet him and tell him how much they admired him and how glad they were to be honored with his friendship. This was soothing; but it could hardly obliterate from his mind the thought that he had retired a second time from executive office with the sharpest criticism of great masses of people upon his administration. In 1781 it had been Henry and these very up-country people who hounded him; now it was New England and the northern interests. Anyway he was at Monticello, his party was still in power and Virginia

THOMAS JEFFERSON

sat at the head of the council board of the nation; his work had not been in vain, and there was never a more buoyant and elastic spirit than that which animated Thomas Jefferson and carried him through so many crises. He took up his daily round of study, of riding over his great plantation and conversing with the friends who came in such numbers that his large house was hardly large enough to contain them. Henceforth he was the "Sage of Monticello."

V

Only one other American has enjoyed the real distinction of being a national "sage" and that one was Andrew Jackson, not one of the three great southern men who, more than all others, had in their hands the making of the South which fought for independence in 1861. Jefferson contributed the idealistic democracy which grew to conservatism under Calhoun, who always insisted that he was a follower of the first Republican president but who nevertheless made slavery the basis of his system, "the stone rejected of the builders" thus becoming head of the corner, while Jefferson Davis, advancing yet a step further, set the world in arms on behalf of slavery—the property interests, the "privileged interests" of the time. It was a long and a deflected road from Jefferson to Jefferson Davis; but the South traveled it and thought it the king's highway, just as the great Republican party has traveled from Lincoln to McKinley, thinking the way perfectly plain and easy—a development almost identical with that of the Democrats from Jackson to Buchanan, from liberty and equality to privilege and property. But let us see how the progress began. Madison was left in Washington to relieve and modify Jefferson's work, to please New England if he could. He gave up the Embargo, but could not bring England or France to any reasonable agreement; and within a short two years he was at the threshold of war. There was no help for it and the great mass of Jefferson's followers joined in the clamor for the conflict—a conflict which the South proposed to wage on behalf of New England and New England's rights! Jefferson thought if war came the Americans would capture Canada,

Florida and Cuba, indeed those were to be the limits of the empire of freedom. Yet he wrote an English friend that if our countries are at war we need not be, and that it was to the interest of both England and the United States to be the closest of friends. Once again the up-country people of the South, the backwoods men this time of Tennessee and Kentucky, volunteered in good numbers and won whatever of land victories there were. The low-country Republicans like John Taylor of Virginia and Macon of North Carolina blocked the way to war, crying out that republicanism would go to the wall in the military scramble. Jefferson lost as much by the war as he had lost by the Embargo; democracy was expensive to him.

But a more interesting phase of Jefferson's life during the seventeen years of retirement at Monticello was his steady loyalty to the idealism of his younger years. His hostility to the Virginia constitution—one of the most unjust in the country—was creditable to him. It will be remembered that the privileged interests of Virginia had defeated him in 1776 when they threw out his constitutional program; they succeeded in distributing the representation of the two great sections in such a way as to secure for the next half century an overwhelming majority for the small eastern counties over the great and populous counties of the West. Reaction followed this victory of the slaveholding part of the state and instead of a progressive and expanding democracy we find Virginia becoming more and more a government of a privileged class. Public schools were wanted in the West but the eastern men opposed all such except as they might be supported locally; the West asked for highways which would give them markets, but the East forbade them; the West believed in universal suffrage, the East formed a restricted electorate; and the West opposed a system of representation which secured to property the control of local law-making and of the federal policy of the state as well, while the majority of the people, mainly farmers, remained helpless.

In 1783 and again in 1794 when Jefferson had urged upon Virginia a revisal of her fundamental law which would have done away with these inequalities and broken down the power of the oligarchy which dominated the state, much to its own hurt and the injury of the nation at large, Henry had always been the chief obstacle in the way of this reform, strange as it may seem; the reason of this opposition was not simply Henry's hatred of Jefferson, but an inveterate hostility on the part of most of the counties south of the James where Henry lived. However, in 1816 the old reformer takes up the matter near his heart in his accustomed way, by urging upon some one else the leadership of the fight which he will support with all his influence.

Between 1776 and 1816 one of those gradual changes, so common in the history of political parties, had been accomplished. Jefferson's followers had in the earlier years of this period favored equal representation of all classes of people in the legislature; he and they had favored above all else the overthrow of slavery, and the party was numerous, if not sufficiently powerful to overcome the opposition or the inertia of the East. In 1800 when the great leveling campaign had been fought in national politics Virginia was overwhelmingly Jeffersonian, but less radical than in 1776 when the fires of liberalism and patriotism were burning briskly. After 1800 the county leaders of the party in Virginia and in the South as well steadily and regularly taught their property-holding followers that Jefferson was not so radical as had been thought. Was he not a slaveholder? Was he not the master of the finest estate in Virginia? How could he believe in the doctrine that all men are equal; certainly he was no longer hostile to slavery. Federalists were told again and again during the Jefferson and Madison administrations that their property (negroes) would not be attacked by the leaders of the Republican party. There are frequent promises of this sort in the addresses of local meetings in Virginia. And Madison was openly proclaimed the conservative. Men who had hated Jefferson voted for Madison as a conservative and former Federalist. Chief Justice Marshall, the strongest defender of slavery, was greatly tempted to vote for Madison, though he managed to hold his ground and not cast a vote in a national election from 1800, when John

Adams had his support, till 1824 when John Quincy Adams was a candidate. The Republicanism of Madison was highly respectable in Virginia; many old eastern families supported it and easily defended their attitude. But real Jeffersonians like John Taylor who believed in reform, like Nathaniel Macon, a pioneer in character, were disposed to eschew the little man in the White House.

During the years of change the county courts which had been suppressed in Virginia in 1770 came once again to dominate Virginia life—but the county courts were Jeffersonian, that is, the county judges belonged to the Republican party and they governed Virginia in a patriarchal way as all Virginians love to be governed. Jefferson said of them: "The justices of the inferior courts are self-chosen, for life, and perpetuate their own body in succession forever, so that a faction once possessing themselves of the bench of a county can never be broken up, but hold their county in chains, forever indissoluble. Yet these justices are the real executive as well as judiciary, in all minor and most ordinary concerns. They tax us at will; fill the office of sheriff, the most important of all the executive officers of the county; name nearly all our military leaders, which leaders, once named, are removable but by themselves. The juries, our judges of all fact, and of law when they choose it, are not selected by the people, nor amenable to them. Where then is our republicanism (democracy) to be found? . . . The true foundation of republican government is the equal right of every citizen, in his person and property, and in their management."[1]

What Jefferson here says was meant to apply to Virginia in 1816; but it applied any time between 1800 and 1850. The county courts practically chose the candidates, for the legislature; these, whether Whig or Democratic made little difference, when elected, selected the governor and the judges of the higher courts, chose United States senators and created districts and counties —units of representation—when they thought it wise to do so. A majority of the courts were located in the East in 1816 as in 1800, in 1850

[1] *Works of Thomas Jefferson* (Ford's Fed. Ed.) XII, 5-7.

as in 1820, for the legislature took good care that the western counties, no matter how populous that section, should never come to power. This condition of things Jefferson, the old man of 1816, declared to be iniquitous; he had said the same when he was a young visionary writing the Declaration of Independence. His remedy was: "Reduce your legislature to a convenient number for full but orderly discussion. Let every man who fights or pays excise have his just and equal right in their selection. Submit them to approbation or rejection (the recall ?) at short intervals. Let the executive be chosen in the same way, and for the same term, by those whose agent he is to be; . . . divide the counties into wards of such size as that every citizen can attend, when called on, and act in person. Ascribe to them the government of their wards in all things relating to themselves exclusively. A justice, chosen by themselves, in each, a constable, a military company, a patrol, a school, the care of their poor. . . . These wards, called townships in New England, are the vital principle of their governments, and have proved themselves the wisest invention ever devised by the wit of man for the perfect exercise of self-government, and for its preservation." He concludes this remarkable letter[1] by urging universal suffrage, equal representation, popular election of governors and judges and periodical amendments to the constitution.

When one remembers what such a program would have meant for Virginia in 1816 one's surprise increases that an old man, the owner of a hundred slaves and the master of thousands of acres of land—an ex-president of the nation—could have urged it. Simple democracy not republicanism, is what he advocated; and democracy would have been as hostile to slavery as it was to the unfair system of representation sustained by the constitution of Virginia.

This letter had hardly reached the hands of the up-country men before it was being copied and circulated preparatory to their coming demonstration, August, 1816, against the old order and the eastern oligarchy. It was not long before its contents reached the ears of eastern leaders

[1] To Samuel Kercheval, the up-country historian.

like Giles and Littleton W. Tazewell; and a commotion was raised about the ears of the "Man of the Mountain" which greatly pleased Chief Justice Marshall who always manifested delight when his life-long enemy found himself sharply criticized. True to his nature Jefferson wrote a second and a third letter beseeching Kercheval, after the manner of a girl in her teens, never more to show his letter nor to allow copies. He was an old man who loved his ease; he was willing to be governed by the little oligarchies, the county courts, or the one-sided legislature, during the remnant of years that remained to him. It is almost pitiful to note the sensitiveness of this able statesman but thorough-going democrat. He had given out a bit of his daily thought to his beloved Virginia and Virginia was suddenly divided into two camps as in the days when he and Patrick Henry were leading the great revolt. He had proposed what would have revolutionized Virginia and made civil war unnecessary in the nation; but the dominant section of the Old Dominion was not the open-minded community he thought it ought to be. The people of the

East were no longer levelers, revolutionists, democrats, even if they had ever been such. The Federalists had metamorphosed the party which Jefferson had founded. Chief Justice Marshall more nearly represented that party than did Jefferson himself. He stood for property; Jefferson for human rights as of old—and there could be no harmony between such men.

The up-country democrats had their meeting: they read Jefferson's advice, and demanded a new constitutional convention. But no eastern county joined them and few of the great black counties sent delegates. A line drawn from Washington City to Danville, Virginia, would have been a sort of Mason and Dixon's line on either side of which dwelt hostile camps. The legislature, still dominated by the slavery counties, which heard the next winter, 1816-17, the cry of the populous and growing West, "stood pat", to use a modern term, and paid no more heed to Jefferson's advice than had the party of reaction in the days when Jefferson sent to Williamsburg his constitution, yet almost every member of that body professed to be ardent followers of the

"Sage of Monticello"—all were Republicans! Not until after Jefferson's death was there a serious effort to give Virginia a just constitution.

VI

Had Jefferson and his friends been successful in 1816 in their reform movement slavery would have disappeared in Virginia by state action. The up-country was then and remained until 1850 hostile to the "institution" and a legislature which they dominated would almost certainly have brought about its gradual overthrow. In fact this was the chief source of opposition on the part of the West to the constitution. Jefferson himself was actuated by this motive.

But Virginia was becoming wedded to slavery and the form of society which it produced during the first and second decades of the nineteenth century, and slavery had fastened itself firmly upon the vitals of the middle counties which had not been the case in 1776. The East had moved westward by two tiers of counties since Jefferson first laid his axe at the root of the noxious tree of privilege. Besides Virginia enjoyed an increased representation in congress by reason of slavery and this had come to be appreciated as fully as it had been by South Carolina and Georgia when they made it a condition to their entering the union in 1787-88. Virginia had then been indifferent to this compromise of the constitution; but now her leaders had come to agree with the lower South on this point. Again Virginia slave-owners were migrating to Alabama and Mississippi in great numbers and founding there new pro-slavery commonwealths; many others bought plantations in the new cotton country and stocked them with slaves but continued to live in the Old Dominion, all of which tended to fasten slavery upon the old commonwealth. Besides the inter-state slave trade had grown to be a good business. The Chief Justice of Virginia had been willing in 1815 to buy a "likely negro" for sale to the southward and William B. Giles had come to reckon the export slave trade as one of the great economic resources of Virginia. Before 1832 the majority of the public men of Virginia acknowledged the force of this economic argument and definitely accepted slavery as a blessing

THOMAS JEFFERSON

not to be interfered with from within or without.

Still Jefferson did not yield. Not a year passed without a lament from him that his work of 1776 had been "nipped in the bud." In 1814 he wrote:[1] "Yet the hour of emancipation is advancing, in the march of time. It will come; and whether brought on by the generous energy of our own minds; or by the bloody process of St. Domingo, excited and conducted by the power of our present enemy [Great Britain], if once stationed permanently within our country, and offering asylum & arms to the oppressed, is a leaf of our history not yet turned over." The next year: "That it [emancipation of the slaves] may finally be effected, and its progress hastened, will be the last and fondest prayer of him who now salutes you." And to Fanny Wright he said that the usual arguments in defense of slavery had no basis in fact, that the negro would prove equal to his own preservation if set free. George McDuffie of South Carolina advanced the doctrine in 1825 that slavery was

[1] *Works of Thomas Jefferson* (Ford's Fed. Ed.) XI, 417; ibid 471.

right and that one man could rightfully possess himself of the faculties of another without his consent. To this Jefferson replied in one of the last letters he ever wrote that he sharply dissented, that he retained his early principles on the subject; but that he was opposed to interference with slavery by the federal government.[1]

These were the ideas of the retired statesman. He never yielded his hostility to "the institution"; he was always solicitous lest some catastrophe come upon the South because of it, and he inspired his grandson, Thomas Jefferson Randolph, with the great plan of emancipation which was presented to the Virginia legislature in 1831, five years after his death. Under the stimulus of the Nat Turner insurrection the Virginia assembly discussed this scheme for months, and at one time it seemed that the great work, gradual emancipation, would be inaugurated. By a single vote the grand committee, appointed to devise a plan, returned an adverse report. The leaders of the southern counties, where slavery was deeply rooted, won the day and lived to urge secession

[1] *Works of Thomas Jefferson* (Ford's Fed. Ed.) XII, 469.

THOMAS JEFFERSON

in 1861 as a further means of perpetuating their power and preserving their favorite property.

Jefferson's influence had thus been strong enough to bring his great old state to the very threshold of the wisest movement ever inaugurated there. Still it failed. Upper and western Virginia had failed again; and property interests, then as usual, maintained the upper hand as against human and personal rights. A new prophet now came forth; Thomas R. Dew, the President of William and Mary College, spoke for Virginia when he ridiculed the Declaration of Independence[1] and proceeded to prove that all men are not equal. From 1832 to 1861 Jefferson's name was not fondly emblazoned on the party standards of Virginia except as he had stood for states rights; his real idealism, the work of his life, was repudiated. And what Virginia assented to South Carolina proclaimed from the housetops and from the sacred desk —Jefferson was a failure. Few states or communities ever made so momentous or fatal a mistake as did Virginia at this crisis. John G.

[1] *Pro-Slavery Argument*, 255 (Ed. of 1852).

Birney was then in northern Alabama working for abolition and pointing his followers to the example of the glorious Old Dominion as she threw off the yoke, for he thought the decision would be for emancipation; the Kentucky abolitionists were expecting the old Mother State to deliver the great blow to the institution which was then fixing itself upon the young and sturdy West. Theodore Weld and John Rankin of Ohio thought the day of their successful preaching was dawning. Verily, the nation would have been saved the awful struggle of 1861 to 1865 and the democracy which Jefferson foreshadowed in his famous Declaration might really have come into being. But Virginia and the South, not the North, decided otherwise.

This little sketch of our greatest American idealist would not be complete without a word as to the sorrows of his last years. When he left the White House in 1809 he was compelled to borrow some thousands of dollars to meet the expenses of his household while president. A friend, Mr. Venable of Virginia, and President Madison, endorsed for him at the United States bank in Washington. During the second war with England he sold some property in Richmond for his friend, Philip Mazzei, the Italian agent of Virginia in Europe during the Revolution, the proceeds of which amounted to some six thousand dollars. Holding the money till the end of the war in order to save it for his friend, he invested it. But his own financial affairs became so pressing by this time that he continued to hold this money and pay interest to Mazzei or his heirs. Thus his debts waxed from year to year.

Owing many thousand dollars already, the war of 1812 made matters worse by destroying his market for tobacco, leaving his many slaves a burden to him. At the end, two fat years of commerce and fair markets were followed by the severe financial panic which well-nigh ruined Virginia. Land lost more than half its value. Jefferson thought he could hardly get more than the amount of a single year's rent for his best tracts in 1819. His debts enlarged relatively and absolutely. It was impossible to meet the obligations which came upon him; but in 1819 his friend Wilson Cary Nicholas for whom he was security in the sum of $20,000 failed and Jefferson was compelled to sell lands to meet these unexpected but inexorable obligations. The Master of Monticello, through no fault of his own, was thus burdened with a load of debt that would have staggered the best of managers and Jefferson was not a good manager.

From the first year of his retirement thousands of people of all grades, from the Marquis LaFayette to the new-made congressman from a western or southern state, visited Monticello. There were no hotels in Charlottsville worthy the name but Jefferson was good enough Virginian to keep "open house" and always to invite his guests to dinner. Men and women and children availed themselves of the hospitality of the great ex-president; they came by tens and dozens and frequently remained weeks at a time. The Duke of Saxe-Weimar and his following cost Jefferson a handsome sum; LaFayette spent several days at Monticello in 1824 when the auctioneer's hammer was already raised for the final fall. From 1815 to 1826 it was a constant stream of guests coming and going at all seasons. When the University of Virginia was being built, the trustees held their meetings with him; politicians like Clay and Crawford stopped on the way to and from Washington. Young George Ticknor, about to set out for Europe in pursuit of his studies, spent a week at Monticello in 1815; and Edward Everett was doubly welcome for his fine bearing and good conversation.

Under these increasing burdens, Jefferson first asked Congress to buy his library which had cost him a hundred thousand dollars; Congress offered twenty-four thousand and received the prize. Thus began in thrift our great national library. But this scarcely stayed the auctioneer's hammer. He next turned to the Virginia legislature asking for the privilege of selling most of his estate by lottery—a way of raising money still common in that part of the country. It was an affecting petition which he sent to this assembly, composed largely of men whose political fortunes had depended at one time or another upon him and his work. He enumerated modestly his sacrifices for the state and nation; he told of the offices he had held and of the bitter conflict he had been compelled to pass through when the Federalists had been overthrown. He went so far even as to remind them of his efforts to overthrow slavery in Virginia! "If," he concluded, "permitted to sell in this way, all will be honestly and honorably paid, I can save the house at Monticello, and a farm adjoining, end my days and bury my bones. If not, I must sell house and all here and carry my family to Bedford, where I have not even a log hut to put my head into."[1]

Jefferson's appeal would have been received with warmer sympathy by the legislators if he had omitted all reference to his reform work. His ideals were not the ideals of the men who directed Virginia affairs in 1826. The party which he had organized and led to victory in 1800 had come to be the very bulwark of conservatism, the guarantee of "things as they are," not as they ought to be. But Jefferson was an old man, a hero of Revolutionary days and much was allowed him. Some opposition was offered; opposition which threatened even to deny him his

[1] *Works of Thomas Jefferson* (Ford's Fed. Ed.) XII, 451.

request, but his personal friends were many and after some delay which gave him much distress, a bill was passed providing for the sale of Thomas Jefferson's estates by means of a lottery!

The tale of his distress, and the way he became involved, spread abroad and soon a public subscription was made up and the money forwarded to his friends. He was much gratified to find so many people, especially in the North, ready to repay some of the sacrifices which he had made on behalf of the general good. The great estate was not sold during its owner's lifetime. The creditors did not push their demands until after Jefferson's death in July following, when it was found that the lottery had not been successful, and men ceased their subscriptions or refused to pay after the great old man was dead. The beautiful and valuable estate of Monticello which had been the "handsomest in America" was sold for less than a third of its real value and Jefferson's debts were not paid from the receipts of his property, but from the pockets of his loyal and devoted executors. It was a poor showing. A property which had once yielded ten to fifteen thousand a year had not been sufficient to maintain one of the simplest of all our great men, and the only daughter of the ex-president was left to the tender mercies of kinspeople or the cold charity of the great outside world. But the South Carolina legislature made an appropriation of ten thousand dollars to Martha Jefferson Randolph, which enabled her to take her family to Washington and live in a barely respectable way, where she had formerly been "first lady of the land."

Jefferson's death was as dramatic as his life had been eventful. On the fiftieth anniversary of the Declaration of Independence, both he and his friend and co-worker of 1776, John Adams, gave up whatever was left of life, each thinking that the other survived. The country and the world noted the strange coincidence and were convinced that God had ordered the end as He had perhaps directed all along the remarkable careers of these chosen leaders of a new nation.

FROM RADICALISM TO
CONSERVATIVE
REVOLT

JOHN C. CALHOUN

I

NOT many of us know John C. Calhoun as he was, as he lived and moved among Americans of the last century. No political party looks back to Calhoun as its founder or rejuvenator, no group of public men proclaim allegiance to his doctrines, no considerable group of individuals outside of South Carolina profess any love for his name and ideals. While all parties seek to find in Jefferson's writings justification for their programs, none dare admit their present policy to be even remotely descended from the teaching of the great Carolinian; yet Calhoun had the approval while a young man of the great Virginian and died more beloved by a greater number of Americans than even the Sage of Monticello. When Jefferson died Virginia wept, but not loudly; when Calhoun's body was carried to Charleston in April, 1850, the whole state mourned as though each man had lost his father. For weeks the ordinary course of business was interrupted and months afterward men talked gloomily as they met upon the streets of Charleston. Only twice in the history of the country have men felt so keenly the loss of one of their leaders—December, 1799, and April, 1864.

It was a simple life that Calhoun led, yet tragedy played with him as with its true child, and a tragic fate awaited in 1850 those who saw the grave close over his mortal remains; and to-day the people of a great state think of him as of no other American and linger sadly about the tomb where their fathers laid him—a people who still feel more keenly than all others the weight of Sherman's terrible blows in 1864 and 1865, who still insist that their cause and his was just.

Like Jefferson, Calhoun came from the plain people. His father and mother were Scotch, whose fathers and mothers came to the country as poor immigrants just a half century before the Revolution. They traversed the mountains and hills of the South from Pennsylvania to Georgia in search of a place to build their cabin.

JOHN C. CALHOUN

And they settled finally in the up-country of South Carolina and there fought the Indians in many a severe struggle both giving and taking the hardest blows. Calhoun's grandmother was killed by the savages while his uncle was murdered by Tories during the Revolutionary war; and all the members of the family of the two generations which preceded John were engaged in an endless struggle with nature for the meager requirements of their frugal habits.

Young Calhoun, born in the year following Yorktown, surrounded by strife and famine and bloodshed, knew none of the pleasures which boys of our day think only their just portion. There were many slaves in South Carolina, but only one or two in the Calhoun family, and as soon as our hero was large enough he was put to the hard tasks of frontier farm life. But manifesting much native alertness, he was sent at the age of twelve, to live in the family of his brother-in-law, a Presbyterian preacher, to learn something of books. He read so much and so closely that his health seemed to be undermined, and his father took him home; and from his thirteenth to his nineteenth year he daily followed the plow alongside his father or the negro slave, Sawney. It was decided that he might try books again and he went to live a second time with his brother-in-law who was now the head of a large "log college," as the backwoods schools were called a hundred years ago.

This log college was not such an institution as Jefferson attended. There was no light-heartedness in this Latin school of the wilderness where the boys lived in small cabins, chopped their own firewood, rose with the sun each day and, studying the ancient classics from morn till night, rested only on the Sabbath. The teacher was a stern master whose purpose was to build anew in his adopted country the kirk of his Scotch fathers, and right well did he perform his task except that many of his pupils became great lawyers rather than great divines. Calhoun and James L. Petigru and George McDuffie were all of the same school.

Two years of Latin and Greek in the South Carolina forest school were sufficient to enable Calhoun to enter the junior class at Yale, his chosen college, and he finished the course two

JOHN C. CALHOUN

years later with the highest honors. At Yale the life was stern, Puritanical and cold; and so was Calhoun. In no sense could he be compared to Jefferson at William and Mary where the boy was ever ready to join the gay life of the community; there was no gaiety in New Haven as there had been none in the South Carolina which Calhoun had known. But instead of "falling in" with the political ways of New England and its proud Federalism, the young Carolinian resisted firmly whatever influence he felt and was disposed to debate even with President Dwight the cause of Thomas Jefferson his *beau ideal* in politics.

From Yale to a good Federalist law school at Litchfield, Connecticut, he next went as though to beard the lion in his den, for his law teachers were such good opponents of the Jefferson régime that they were urging New England to secede from the unholy union with the Virginia Delilah, and make a country of their own[1] and a government after their own hearts. Calhoun drank deep of the learning of New England but not of its spirit. He returned to South Carolina to

[1] Gaillard Hunt's *Life of Calhoun*, p. 15.

continue his study of the law and to begin its practice in 1807. While successful as a lawyer, he had less liking for the profession than had Jefferson, and in a few years he settled down on a farm near the ancestral home in Abbeville district, there to make himself a country gentleman and local leader, a man to guide his neighbors and now and then to represent them in the state legislature.

But two things had happened to influence profoundly the career of the young up-country planter: years ago when his father was a member of the legislature, which then sat in Charleston, he had attended a negro auction and bought a "likely" negro man. It was an unusual thing for an up-country man to do before the opening of the nineteenth century; but the stern Puritan of the frontier yielded to the pressure of aristocratic example in his state, and put his negro, Adam, upon the horse with himself and journeyed home. From that day Adam and not Calhoun dominated the family thoughts. Adam fixed the destiny of the Calhoun children who in turn did much to shape the social life of the up-country.

JOHN C. CALHOUN

Of course Adam must have a wife and soon came the negro family with black Sawney who was given to young John Calhoun as a personal servant. John and Sawney had followed the plow together and together did much of the daily toil inseparable from farm life; the Calhoun homestead was not yet a plantation.

The other event which linked Calhoun to aristocratic South Carolina was his marriage in 1811 to Floride Bonneau Calhoun, a wealthy cousin, who was already identified with the Charleston aristocracy. The Bonneaus were Huguenots of the highest social standing, trained in the traditions of the old colonial families. Their view of life was very different from that of the rough Abbeville district; but, as always in Southern social evolution, the older families readily accepted alliance with the promising and talented members of the lower order and thus renewed their vigor and strength, at the same time consolidating the masses whom it was fashionable nevertheless to regard as inferior. Being identified with slavery and united in marriage to an "old family" Calhoun became an integral part of the best life of his state, plain and democratic as he was in all his tastes and feelings.

Calhoun was a product of the hills, of the people who usually voted against the low country; his father had been looked upon with contempt in Charleston when he ridiculed the federal constitution which in South Carolina as in Virginia was forced upon the state by the great property interests, slavery in particular. The Calhouns were Jeffersonians and of course could not be counted as of the privileged class, yet even Pinckneys and Rutledges had voted for the radical Virginian. So that when young Calhoun settled down as the master of an estate, "Bath" by name, and gradually gathered slaves and horses and a growing family about him, there was no denying him a place in the existing order of things. Besides he had made good his pretensions by going in proper season to Charleston, if not to participate in the races, at least to acknowledge that the gay city had its claims upon all gentlemen.

The year of Calhoun's marriage he "stood for congress" for the lower district of South Carolina as a supporter of a warlike policy against Great

Britain. It was not difficult in 1811 to win sympathy in this region of the South by "twisting the lion's tail," and Calhoun, whose grandmother had been slain by Indians, instigated to the deed by English agents, and whose uncle had been wantonly slain by a Tory, was the proper person to "run" upon a platform of defiance to England. Besides the whole back-country of America had been irritated and angered by the British policy of stirring up troubles on the border and retaining on her pension rolls Indian chiefs whose business it was to prevent the growth of the young republic. It was not love for New England shipping that caused Calhoun or the South to demand a war for sailors' rights, but the desire to be rid of the obstacles which England was constantly putting in the way of building up the West. The West was an ally of the South and every new state established in that region only rendered the more certain the isolation and helplessness of New England. As Calhoun thought in 1811 so thought also Grundy of Tennessee, Clay of Kentucky, and Porter, a westerner, of New York—and indeed most of the men who were returned to congress that year.

With his place in South Carolina fixed, a fair reputation as a leader among his people and a definite program for national action, Calhoun entered congress for the first time in December, 1811. He was twenty-nine years old, full six feet tall, with head and shoulders slightly inclined forward, dark hair which fell down over his temples, and deep set eyes either blue or gray according to his mood, and, withal, an air of commanding intelligence which readily impressed itself upon all who came into touch with him. He was tender, kind-hearted, somewhat abashed as yet when in the presence of the great, rustic rather than polished in manner; he was unaccustomed to drink or carousing, pure-minded as a woman but unromantic, never having read a volume of poetry in his life nor thought out a rhyme even during the days of his courtship with Floride Bonneau, his wife. But this modesty and even country plainness did not indicate absence of will or lack of energy sufficient to make his influence felt in any gathering. Calhoun was the equal of any of the great men who

JOHN C. CALHOUN

entered congress on that eventful first Tuesday in December, as the country was soon to learn.

And this latent power and boundless energy of mind was at the service, like Jefferson's, of the plain back-country people who were beginning to see what their rôle in national politics might be; he was ready to speak for democracy which then meant national power and self-respect. It was the West which had brought Jefferson to power in 1800; the West now sent to Washington the vigorous young men who were to rebuke Jefferson and his successor and friend, Madison, for not asserting the national spirit as against the brutal and overbearing conduct of Great Britain. It was not slaveholding South Carolina which spoke in Calhoun; nor was it the timid property interests that had spoken in the last elections—but the people restive under the restraints of older and more conservative leaders.

The South Carolina group in congress during our second war with England was almost as remarkable as that from the up-country of Virginia in 1800 when Jefferson, Madison, Monroe and Marshall all hailed from the same neighborhood of the Old Dominion. William Lowndes, Langdon Cheves and John C. Calhoun were not so fortunate as the men who composed the Virginia dynasty; but they were quite as able and one of them was destined to attain a fame as great as any of the Virginians save Jefferson alone. The three South Carolinians were all young men, all Republicans and from the same section of their state—a sort of up-country product. Clay, the speaker, was embarrassed by the ability of his friends from South Carolina. Notwithstanding the complaints of some, the great committees, naval, appropriations and foreign relations, were guided and directed by them, and when Calhoun suggested that, since he was the youngest member from his state, his name be dropped as member of the committee on foreign relations, the new chairman, Smiley of Pennsylvania, resigned in order that Calhoun, the second member, might not thus escape the position which his abilities suggested.

The development of the South under Jefferson and the Virginia dynasty had been rapid. Population had poured into Kentucky, Tennessee and other Mississippi communities; the back-country of the nation had fallen to the portion of the South. Western men everywhere were supporters of the Democratic-Republican program. But the leadership of this expanding, restless South was fast shifting from Virginia to South Carolina; and economic supremacy had already departed from the Old Dominion. South Carolina exports in 1810 totaled $10,600,000 while those of Virginia had fallen to $4,500,000. Moreover tobacco, the great Southern staple, had given place to cotton of which $15,000,000 worth had been grown during the same year. South Carolina was the land of cotton, and the up-lands, not the proud and domineering Tidewater, were reaping the rich harvests.

It was not unnatural then that the most powerful group in Congress in 1811 should hail from the Palmetto state and that the very existence of the Virginia dynasty should depend on the good will of South Carolina and Kentucky. The militant reformers of 1800 had become conservative before 1811 and a majority of Jefferson's followers had become what would to-day be called "stand-patters." They were not nationalists and they did not feel the sting of English insult. Their opponents, the Federalists or New England leaders, failed likewise to recognize the rising spirit of the people. If New England had been nationalist an alliance with the West might easily have given them control of the country and a new lease of political power. But they failed and never again were Federalists to occupy the coveted places at the national council board.

The younger Republicans disgusted with their own party and with the men whom they had been accustomed to call great, like the insurgents of our time, Democratic as well as Republican, formulated a program of their own and forced it upon a halting and trembling administration. They gave Madison and Monroe, the Virginians of the old school, the option of declaring war upon England in defense of the new nationalism and on behalf of a militant Southern and Western imperialism or of yielding the leadership of the country which had come to them from Jefferson. It gave the Virginians much agony of soul to make the choice but they were not long in doubt which horn of the dilemma to seize. With the administration in their hands the insurgents found little difficulty in bringing Congress around to their view. Thus Calhoun and Clay and Grundy became the most powerful governing element of the rejuvenated party and the West and South proceeded to punish England by taking from her the long coveted Canada and the lucrative fur trade of the "western waters." The war was a failure from the start and many a time during the years of 1813 and 1814 young men like Clay were about to go to the front to make good their bold promises. After many rebuffs, the failure of all the efforts against Canada and the direst distress among the people, the struggle came almost by accident to a close without loss of territory. The older politicians, the Federalists, who came near regaining control more than once during these years, retired finally and the younger men chastened by disaster were given the field. Theirs was the task of reconstruction and of building well the foundations of the nation which they had insisted had been in existence from the beginning. The opportunity was not unlike that which came to Washington and Hamilton in 1789 or to the Republican leaders in 1866.

Aside from the war policy of 1812, Calhoun's name is not associated particularly with any of the events of the time before 1816 when the work of reconstruction was to be done. It was at that time that Calhoun's genius as a leader of men and a political philosopher of the greatest importance became known to the country. The leadership, the initiative of the time, was in the House of Representatives, the President and Cabinet practically abdicating, and Calhoun, after Clay, was the first man in the House group.

It had been an alliance of the South and West which supported the war policy, and western and southern communities had furnished the recruits for the armies and the leaders for the campaigns. Now that the war had come to an end, this alliance was expected to solve the problems entailed by the war. And what was clearly the greatest work of the time was the leveling of the Alleghanies. The war had shown above all else that easy communication between Washington and Pittsburg, Richmond and Cincinnati was the great national problem and, politically, the removal of this difficulty would make the union of South and West permanent and render the opposition of New England harmless. It was not a question for constitutional hairsplitting, but a practical matter that must be met at the peril of national existence. The policy of protection and home markets, of finance and banking, was secondary.

It was in this light, at least, that Calhoun viewed the matter of internal improvements and consequently we find him taking the lead in this work—in making great highways and canals which should make markets for Kentucky and the Northwest in Baltimore, Richmond and Charleston, and bind the seacoast people to their kindred in the great interior. "I speak not for South Carolina, but the nation," was his open defiance to those who would put states rights and local advantage before his large scheme. What he desired was so to unite the interests and sections of the country that a second Hartford convention would offer no terrors, and his method was to apply or expand national powers in a way that would enable the government to overcome the great mountain barriers. To find money for the accomplishment of such an undertaking he was willing to enact tariff laws and even to give protection to American industry against foreign competition, but his fundamental purpose was always to build up the nation against the forces of disintegration so painfully prevalent during the recent crisis.

We have here the key to Calhoun's career—he sees clearly what is needed; he is an ardent patriot and his imagination portrays to him a great and expanding country. In this he was at one with Jefferson who could violate the constitution and his own understanding of his powers as president in order to make room for the future. Calhoun was ready also to ignore the plain terms of the fundamental law if he could carry out his purpose.

But other men felt as did Calhoun. Clay saw the needs of the time and likewise proposed to brush away the cobwebs of law; he was more ardent and more ambitious than Calhoun, and in order to hasten the realization of his ambition as well as his scheme of national greatness, he threw out the bait of a protective tariff for protection's sake and put the stress on building up home markets at the "cost of the foreigner." Clay conceived early of the union of the North and the West, and year after year, until 1824, offered his increasing measure of protection until he won the votes in the House of practically every middle states' man and a majority of the East. Thus the rivalry of the two leaders became patent early in their careers; it was to grow bitter as the years passed until these great men could not exchange friendly greetings when they met on the street or in the Senate.

Monroe offered Calhoun a seat in the cabinet in 1817—the war portfolio—and, though the same position had been refused by Clay, Shelby of Tennessee, and Lowndes, he took it without complaint or condition and, it may as well be said, made the ablest war secretary the Government ever had till Jefferson Davis came to the same office in 1853. While Calhoun was at the council board Clay was speaker of the House and organizing his following, and Jackson, as yet an unsuspected rival for high honors, was silently growing upon the democracy of the West. Clay, a western man, undertook to build upon a system of special privilege and bind the wealthy East and the pioneer West together—the manufacturer and the producer of raw materials; Jackson was making his appeal to the imagination of the plain people of the older states as well; while Crawford, a fellow cabinet member, undertook to mobilize the old Jefferson forces and popularity; and John Quincy Adams had the advantage of being in the line of promotion, as both Madison and Monroe had gone to the presidency from the office of secretary of state. Calhoun watched this "hurdle race" with keen understanding, while his fellows all regarded him as a promising but immature politician. Late in this period of bitter rivalry, all the candidates realized that even Calhoun had been listening to the hum of the presidential bee, and suddenly all turned upon him like the proverbial dogs in the fight for the bone. From that day this "captivating man," as Adams had pronounced him, became most uncaptivating and Calhoun himself never ceased to long for and strive for the presidency. Much of the bitterness of his life and many of the woes of his country, possibly the civil war itself, may be traced directly to the failure of the people to make him chief magistrate.

II

In 1824 Calhoun was as popular in Pennsylvania as was Jackson, and friends in that state were the first to bring forward the South Carolina candidate for the presidency, and he in turn was not averse to assuring manufacturing interests in the North that he was as good a protectionist as Clay or Adams. But Jackson was the idol already of the Southwest, Tennessee, western Georgia, Alabama and Mississippi. The ruthless policy of the hero of New Orleans toward the Indians stimulated the border appetite for new lands, and what delighted the Southwest pleased also the Northwest where the presence of the Indians was as unwelcome as in Georgia. Jackson's fame had been greatly enhanced by his exploits in Florida and he was rather liked for his summary hanging of a few foreigners, especially Englishmen and Spaniards, even if it jeopardized the peace of the country; and the more the older leaders like Clay attacked the bold general the more resolutely the people called for Jackson as their future standard bearer. Nothing was clearer in early 1824 than that Jackson had won the lasting friendship of the West.

As Calhoun was stronger in the older section of the country and especially in the older South, he joined his forces to those of the older candidate, being convinced—and in fact Jackson repeatedly declared that he was too old to run for the presidency—that four years later the West would appreciate his conduct and he would be made president. Thus we have the first understanding, the first practical agreement, whereby the West was to support the South and Calhoun in the presidential game. Calhoun was chosen vice-president, receiving almost unanimous support, while Jackson was, as the rough charges of the day would have it, defrauded of the presidency by a bargain consummated in the House of Representatives between Clay and Adams. This made a new trial of strength between Adams and Jackson certain and Calhoun kept aloof from the conflict though he was regarded as a friend of the

JOHN C. CALHOUN

doughty general. Clay continued his almost disreputable effort to consolidate the North, East and West in his own behalf by urging a tariff as absurdly high as even the wool growers could ask. Calhoun was compelled to sacrifice much of his strength in the North in order to retain even a remnant of his popularity in the South where the opposition to the tariff had become almost fanatical. Still Calhoun was elected vice-president with Jackson as president in 1828 and almost without opposition. He was everywhere regarded as the successor to Jackson in 1832 if only the tariff quarrel should not upset all plans.

However, the way of the politician is as hard as the rewards are sometimes high. Calhoun must bring Jackson to a low tariff view and he must keep his South Carolina people "in hand" until the President could effect the change. But Jackson was not willing to sacrifice his following in Pennsylvania which Clay was hoping he would do in order to please South Carolina. The West, his base of operations, was not aroused about the tariff anyway. On the other hand South Carolina had, even then, a reputation for having things her own way and particularly now that the enemies of Calhoun had such a good chance to punish him for his too broad nationalism. The tomahawk was therefore taken up with vigor in the Palmetto state in 1827-28. William Smith who had been accused of profiting to the extent of $25,000 from Hamilton's funding system, when the former was a member of the House, and who had taken "orders from the Treasury," now came out boldly against Calhoun and all his ways. President Thomas Cooper of the College of South Carolina, who had made so much difficulty for John Adams in 1800, also took up the hatchet. Before the assembly of the legislature of 1828, it seemed that a great majority of the people of the state were ready to repudiate Calhoun. McDuffie and Cheves, both former nationalists, now repudiated what Calhoun had so long stood for. The Vice-President's one redeeming act had been his deciding vote in the Senate in 1827, which defeated the tariff bill of that year.

Calhoun's ambition for the presidency was indeed about to encounter rough sailing; his political existence was even in the greatest danger. How could he stem the tide?

Such a crisis as this had been evident perhaps to astute men from the beginning, for he had always to reckon upon an alliance of the South and West, and the West, in the nature of things, must favor a tariff in order to secure to the national government the revenue to build her highways to eastern markets; besides Kentucky and Ohio and even Indiana and Illinois were not averse to a high tariff on commodities which they did not consume, and which was supposed to secure them a high price for their hides. The Clay scheme of a union between the West and the North was now as natural as had been the similar coöperation of the South and West in Jefferson's day. The two sections, however friendly, could not work together now that the South had come to oppose almost unanimously the so-called "American system" which Clay had long advocated.

South Carolina, to make matters worse, was hastening along the road which led to revolution when the whole country would be against her.

Her remedy for the tariff was refusal to obey the law; the port of Charleston was to decline to pay the customs which the federal law exacted. This meant war. To prevent this Calhoun cast himself into the breach. He wrote the *South Carolina Exposition* of 1828 which the legislature adopted as the language of the state without giving out the name of the distinguished author. The *Exposition* found a way to nullify national law without violating the constitution! The state, all states, had a reserved right to refuse obedience to so-called national laws enacted in violation of the national constitution and the state, not the federal courts, was to decide when a law was unconstitutional! This was what South Carolina desired, for, though her people are and were then brave as any in the world, war with the federal government was not sought. Meanwhile Calhoun was to do what "in him lay" to hasten Jackson's favorable action on the tariff, while the people of the state refrained from all hostile movements until he had ample time to move. Calhoun was thus the link between Columbia and Washington, the only guarantee of peace

JOHN C. CALHOUN

in South Carolina. It was a fearful responsibility but Calhoun was compelled to assume it; yet all his good intentions proved unavailing. The right and patriotic course was the one Calhoun selected and had this course been followed Calhoun must have succeeded Jackson as president and South Carolina would not have risked nullification. An evil day it was that broke the friendly feeling between the President and the Vice-President, and a still more unfortunate one when Clay in 1832, declared he would have his high tariff increased once more, against "the South, the Democratic party, and the devil."[1]

Calhoun held impetuous South Carolina in tow from 1828 to 1832, and this was a feat which not only showed the great power of the man but his love for the nation. What he hoped to do was to bring congress to a reasonable tariff, say a general average of 20%, with which all the South would have been pleased and which would have been ample protection to Northern manufactures, and then, attaining the leadership of the country, go on with the great nationalizing work of knit-

[1] McMaster: *History of the United States*, VI, 135.

ting the South and West together. And in view of what the tariff has done for us and of Calhoun's unequaled influence and power as shown in after years, who will say this was not the correct course? It had been the union of the South and West which sustained Jefferson's administrations; coöperation of South and West was still the basis of the national policy; and there are those among us to-day who look for a solution of our twentieth century troubles only from a friendly understanding between these really democratic sections of the country.

But the sweets of high office proved very appetizing to Jackson. He did not feel so old at the end of his term as when he had first been named for president by his friend, William B. Lewis, in 1823. And when Van Buren, the "boss" of New York, who had become almost necessary to the Administration, persuaded the New York *Courier* and *Enquirer* to call for a second term, he did not peremptorily decline to be a candidate. Calhoun's paper, *The National Telegraph,* opposed at once the New York proposition as premature. A newspaper controversy followed which must have aroused suspicions in the mind of the President. In March, 1830, Lewis drafted a petition, asking the President to "stand a second time" and sent it to a friend in Pennsylvania. The document came to Washington in due time signed by sixty-eight politicians and prominent characters with no hint that its origin was not in the Keystone state. The "spontaneous" call from the great state of Pennsylvania was soon published in the leading papers of the country. Calhoun's suspicions were now aroused and he gave out word among his friends that the "old hero" must be opposed, and the Pennsylvania legislature refused to endorse unanimously the "spontaneous" call. But New York, by the same process of diligent cultivation, added the weight of her growing numbers to the demand that the President "sacrifice himself" for the party and the country. Calhoun was outclassed.

Meanwhile, however, Van Buren's friend, James A. Hamilton, son of Alexander Hamilton, had visited Georgia seeking to pacify William H. Crawford, bitter enemy of both Jackson and Calhoun. He learned there that Crawford, whom

Jackson credited with having sought to have him punished for his high-handed conduct in Florida in 1819, had not opposed the General on that occasion but that Calhoun was the man who had done the fatal deed. With evidence of this in his possession, Hamilton consulted Lewis. Lewis, wise man that he was, kept his information eighteen months until Jackson had reason to suspect the South Carolinian of a "hasty" ambition. Then, as though it were only a small matter, he asked his chief if he had not known all along that Calhoun was his enemy. Astonished at what seemed to be true, Jackson ordered the letter, which Hamilton had brought back from Georgia two years before to be produced. Lewis coached Hamilton not to produce the letter but to secure one from Crawford direct which should settle the question at once.

Lewis' web was not complete and he held back the Georgia evidence. This was in the winter of 1829-30. Calhoun was endeavoring to hold South Carolina back "while he brought Jackson around," and prepared the way for his own succession. He stood as yet for protection in

Pennsylvania and for internal improvements in the West. At this juncture the Peggy O'Neal scandal reached a climax, and all the blame for the trouble about Mrs. Eaton, the former barmaid, now wife of Secretary Eaton of the Cabinet, was laid to Mrs. Calhoun's charge. Mrs. Eaton's reputation in Washington was of the worst; but this would have had no political significance if she had not suddenly become the wife of a member of the Cabinet. In this new rôle she must either be received in Washington society or be "snubbed." Since her husband was a Tennesseean and very intimate with the President, the latter alternative was exceedingly dangerous for any "Cabinet lady." Jackson was warned early of the coming storm; but storms either social or otherwise had no terrors for "Old Hickory." He decided to break a lance for Mrs. Eaton whom he declared to be as pure as fresh-driven snow, and woe to any one who opposed him.

Mrs. Calhoun came from an old Charleston family, and any one who has any knowledge of the Charleston aristocracy knows that no lady who hailed from that proud city would for a moment allow a Tennessee backwoods man to dictate to her in matters social, even if a husband's political fortunes were at stake. Mrs. Calhoun was the wife of the Vice-President. She was the most popular woman in Washington and her husband was the most popular man. If Mrs. Calhoun refused to recognize Mrs. Eaton it would be very doubtful whether any other lady in the city would "know" her. And Mrs. Calhoun refused to recognize Mrs. Eaton and declined to take any suggestions, if any were offered, from her distinguished husband. The gauntlet was thrown down and Jackson hastened to take it up. On September 10, 1829, the President summoned a cabinet meeting to discuss Mrs. Eaton's case and to give his advisers his opinion which was practically a command to compel their ladies to visit the unwelcome recruit to Washington official life. Jackson's commands were for once ignored.

With Mrs. Calhoun the chief sinner in this matter, Calhoun's burdens became too great for the ordinary politician to bear—though Calhoun was no ordinary politician. The understanding about the succession rested upon the most unstable foundation and all Calhoun's plans for the future depended upon this understanding being carried out. It was an understanding much like that between Jefferson and Madison or Monroe and John Quincy Adams, except that Calhoun, not Jackson, was the greater partner. Never has there been a political agreement between public leaders in this country fraught with more possibility for good than this, and yet this was broken with the utmost disregard of truth and fair dealing.

Nothing shows more clearly the reality of this agreement than the personnel of the Cabinet. The Vice-President had named three members, Ingham, the Secretary of the Treasury, Branch, of the Navy, and Berrien, an anti-Crawford man from Georgia, Attorney-General. The remaining members, Van Buren, Eaton and Barry, the latter a particular enemy of Henry Clay, were attached to the President. The abler men, except Van Buren, were followers of Calhoun; and the great Treasury Department, with its army of important subordinates and many bank officials throughout the country, was held by his most intimate friend.

124 STATESMEN OF THE OLD SOUTH

Under ordinary circumstances the Vice-President must have succeeded and this prospect was fully understood in South Carolina where the angry leaders were able to hold even themselves in restraint.

It was under this high pressure that Calhoun attended the famous dinner on Jefferson's birthday, April 13, 1830, and there heard the famous defiance from his chief which foreboded a complete break-up in the Administration. Jackson offered the toast: "Our Federal Union: It must be preserved." Everyone saw that the shaft was aimed at the Vice-President and no one realized its significance more fully than the ambitious Carolinian. But on May 1, the Crawford letter, applied for six months before, was received. It purported to give a faithful account of what transpired in the Monroe cabinet meeting of 1818 in which Calhoun criticized Jackson's conduct in Florida. The President demanded an explanation of the "perfidy" of having opposed his interests. Jackson could not understand how any man could justly criticize any of his acts and he could not appreciate the honest and

JOHN C. CALHOUN 125

faithful support which Calhoun had later given him. Crawford, who had long been a bitter enemy of the South Carolina leader, had dealt this fatal blow, for with the President's opposition, there could be no chance for him to reach the White House in years to come. When the breach was complete Calhoun's friends resigned from the Cabinet, his paper, the *Telegraph,* was deprived of the support of the Administration and another organ, the *Globe,* was a little later established. Early in 1831 the Administration which Calhoun had done so much to bring into existence and from which he had hoped so much, was rent asunder and the public knew that Calhoun and his friends were banished from court and in the highest disfavor. It was generally thought that the Peggy O'Neal affair had been the cause. Perhaps the first cause of the break had been the changed attitude of the President on the question of the succession. This change had been brought about by the intrigues of Lewis and Van Buren as well as by the love of power which grew upon Jackson with the passing of the years. It was already arranged that he was to have another term, that Van Buren was to succeed with two terms after which Benton of Missouri was to come in for eight years! The combination between the South and West which Jackson represented was not to be followed by a return of Southern men to the presidency but of Northern politicians who had been out of office too long already. The idea was to hold the West and the middle states together and destroy all chance of Clay's success. Van Buren was the only man who could carry on the work after 1837, for he controlled New York and would control Pennsylvania if a sufficiently liberal tariff allowance could be offered. It was natural therefore for Jackson to hate Nullification and denounce the state which he thought had given him his birth.

Calhoun in 1831, like Jefferson in 1798, presided over the Senate and from this throne of power he could checkmate and harass the headstrong President who had taken the bit in his teeth. Clay was returned to the Senate, after the sharpest fight of his life, in 1831, and while the imperious Kentuckian could not love the imperious Carolinian, both had good reason to loathe the "upstart and arrant martinet" of the White House. Before Clay's return to Washington in December, 1831, he had visited the Southwest and in New Orleans, Natchez, Memphis, he was received with an enthusiasm, an outpouring of the popular applause which convinced him that neither Jackson nor Calhoun was the master in that region. Later he received ovations in Ohio and Pennsylvania which remind the student of the great popular demonstrations which have been given in recent years to Bryan and Roosevelt. Clay entered the Senate in 1831, convinced that nothing could prevent his election to the presidency the following autumn.

Calhoun had watched the lower South with less scrutiny than South Carolina. Everywhere opposition to the tariff was growing, becoming almost fanatical in many of the older and more populous sections. At Hampden Sidney College, Virginia, the students resolved unanimously not to wear the "protected" clothing of the North and on commencement occasions in South Carolina and Georgia, men like George McDuffie appeared in homespun while their negro valets wore discarded broadcloth! Was Calhoun to be blamed if he, too, counted on the support of most Southern states? Had not the legislatures of every state from the Potomac to the Mississippi declared the tariff of 1828 both outrageous and contrary to the intentions of the founders of the republic? Calhoun thought that when he chose to make the issue the President and not himself would find public sympathy painfully lacking. And if Clay should join him what might not be done to bring Jackson to his senses.

Still Calhoun was a nationalist. He did not desire to see the issue made, least of all a clash of arms between the South which he thought would be united and the North which might follow an irate President. Hence the effort to bring Clay to an agreement that the tariff should be revised downward. The Kentucky leader was infatuated; he was certain that a high tariff was what the country wanted and that Clay was the most popular man in the nation. The great, uproarous assemblages which greeted him everywhere he went had intoxicated him. No man has ever been more certain of anything not actually realized than was he that Clay would be the next president and that Andrew Jackson would retire to Tennessee in 1833 a wiser if a sadder man.

Calhoun's suggestion that an alliance should be struck, whereby the tariff should go and with it the common enemy, was spurned. The tariff with all its unpopularity was boldly made an issue in 1832, though the question of whether the national bank should be re-chartered was raised by the President and welcomed by Clay.

In the spring of 1832 Calhoun, convinced that the North was joined to its idols and that there was no chance for an "adjustment of the tariff," turned all his great abilities to the "interposition" which he had outlined in 1828 and which South Carolina had been panting to apply. It is unnecessary here to outline the revolutionary course of that impetuous state during the years of 1832 and 1833. The program which Calhoun had sent to the legislature four years before in strictest secrecy had been made known as his, and a great majority of the people accepted the new doctrine without stopping to wonder at the amazing change of front of its author. What Calhoun sought in 1832 and 1833 was absolute unanimity in his state. In this he failed though his majority was overwhelming and from this time till his death the state was to him a willing slave, a pocket borough more unique than that of Henry Clay in Kentucky.

What amazed and chagrined Calhoun after the test of Nullification had been applied, was the failure of the South to respond. Not one state endorsed the new doctrine though Virginia dallied long with the dangerous thing. But if Calhoun was bitterly disappointed at the failure of the South to rise against the tariff, Clay was sore distressed to find that all the enthusiasm of the great popular gatherings which he aroused was only froth. Jackson was reëlected by a majority as unexpected as it was unprecedented. In Louisiana the Clay electors were beaten two to one and in Mississippi where he had spoken to "acres of people" no votes at all were registered for him. Jackson's majority over both Clay and Wirt, who polled almost as many votes as the Kentuckian, was more than 150,000! The "old hero" was overflowing with joy when congress reassembled. The people had punished and

JOHN C. CALHOUN

humbled Clay; he would dispatch Calhoun in the shortest order. Though he had been something of a nullifier in times past he was no nullifier when Calhoun was in that camp.

South Carolina sent her idol to Washington in December, 1832, much after the fashion of the great German Reformer on his way to Worms in 1521. Escorts of devoted followers saw him safe across the border where loyal North Carolinians hailed him as a second Luther; in southern Virginia John Randolph sent him his dying blessing. But in Washington the atmosphere was sadly lacking in warmth and men peered at Calhoun with the sort of curiosity with which they greet great men whose course is thought to lead to ruin, perhaps ignominious death. Clay came on late, as well he might, after the awful blow of the preceding November. He had lost his dictatorial air; his short and ugly saying of the previous session "the South, the Democratic party and the devil" had lost its force. Common men who looked on that winter in Washington might well have wondered whose plight was the worse, that of Calhoun with his state at his heels or Clay repudiated by the nation in a way unknown to American politics.

Instead of the quiet succession to the presidency which Jackson and his friends had promised him in 1828, Calhoun was now threatened with a trial for treason and his state was put under the ban of the empire. But Jackson felt the justice of the cotton growers' complaint against the tariff and he prepared to sweeten the bitter pill which he was making for South Carolina in the form of the famous Force bill. The tariff was to be reduced from an average of about forty per cent to twenty-five per cent. When Clay saw what was about to happen he seized the reins of legislation and "put through" the Senate in almost indecent haste the famous Tariff Reform bill of 1833, accomplishing with the aid of Webster and without great hostility from the protected interests, the same result the President was about to attain. A combination of the friends of Clay, Calhoun and Webster, who was not, however, wholly committed, had been effected and the sturdy old soldier in the White House who had just been reëlected with an unprecedented majority was powerless either to punish Calhoun and South Carolina or reduce the tariff. The Force bill was passed, but South Carolina had already taken steps to avert the blow which was really not much of a blow. Calhoun had won; by his threatened intervention the nation had been brought to terms; the greatest and the extremest protectionist in the country had revised his own defiant tariff of a year before and the manufacturers themselves had yielded!

III

It has been customary in American history-writing to treat Calhoun from 1833 to his death in 1850, as an arch-conspirator, seeking the overthrow of the government which he served and upon which he had bestowed the best years of his life. I am constrained to view him differently. Calhoun was a nationalist at heart to the day of his death and in the intimacy of private correspondence he spoke of a severed nation "bleeding at every pore"—a state of things which he said he could not think of encouraging.[1] What he

[1] Jameson, J. F., *Correspondence of John C. Calhoun,* Am. Hist. Asso. Reports 1899, Vol. II, 391.

was striving for during the last seventeen years of his life was the building of a "solid" South which should follow his teaching implicitly and which, cast into the scales of national politics, would decide all great questions in its favor. And it cannot be doubted that he expected to be elevated to the presidency as a natural result—a position which he coveted as warmly as did Henry Clay himself. It was not his aim to break up the Union but to dominate it.

His method of uniting the people of the South was to show them that without such union the greatest interest of their section, slavery, was doomed. Calhoun sought to weld together his people on a basis of economic interest just as Clay had sought to build a "solid" North on the basis of a high tariff. On this subject parties had ceased to differ in large sections of the North. Rhode Island Democrats were "tariff" Democrats; Pennsylvania made protection a *sine qua non* of coöperation with the party of Jackson; Kentucky, Ohio and the Northwest voted solidly for that policy of the nation which was thought to operate in their favor. The South, regardless of party lines, had come to regard slavery as either a good thing or an evil which could not, and ought not, to be eradicated; Whigs vied with Democrats in asseverating their loyalty to the "peculiar institution." Slavery was uglier in outward appearance than protection, but in principle negro servitude and a protective tariff were alike—each meant the exploitation of the weaker and more ignorant classes of society by the wealthier and more intelligent. As a matter of morals there was no difference between the demand of the Western Reserve that a prohibitive tariff in favor of their wool be maintained by the federal government and that of South Carolina that negro slavery should be forever guaranteed. A high tariff on wool compelled the poor white man to give his labor to others without recompense; slavery compelled the negro to work for his master without reward.

While Calhoun never yielded a hair's breadth on his main program—unity of the slave states—he never failed to reckon upon the support of the growing Northwest where slavery was not unpopular and where hatred and fear of the free negro had become a sort of mania. In Ohio, Indiana, Illinois and Iowa he had ardent and able followers, while half the senators from this region at the time of his death were then or had been owners of negro slaves. With a following, young, ardent and growing, the great South Carolinian laid down his program of national protection to slavery as a constitutional guarantee and on this point it will hardly be denied that he read the great document aright. The idea that slavery was a good thing which the churches ought to defend came easy to him after reading Professor Thomas R. Dew's famous pamphlet of the year 1832.[1]

Dew was the ablest publicist in Virginia, and one of the first in the country, a teacher of political science in William and Mary College, who had spent years in study and travel in Europe, especially in Germany where he had come into touch with the greatest thinkers of the time. He ridiculed the ideas of Jefferson about human equality, slavery and emancipation and he called Virginia's attention to the great advantage

[1] Dew, Thomas R., *Review of the Debates of the Virginia Legislature, 1831-1832*, Richmond, Va., 1832.

of raising negroes for the ever-widening market in the lower South. Virginia should become a great slave-producing state. In this he had been ably seconded by the late governor, William B. Giles, who in 1829 published similar doctrines though not in the philosophical and unanswerable manner of Dew.

Calhoun had prided himself on being a follower of the great Jefferson and he had sought in 1833 to show that Nullification emanated from that revered authority. Jackson on the other hand wrote Nathaniel Macon in 1833 that he would coerce South Carolina in the name of the Sage of Monticello, and the rank and file of the Jackson democracy was certainly Jeffersonian in most of the items of their faith. Calhoun thought, or convinced himself, that Dew was right, that he spoke for the property holding classes in the South and that his arguments must become classic in a land teeming with slaves whose value was enhancing with each passing year. He accepted the teachings of the Williamsburg professor and ever after preached the same doctrine; but he did not think it necessary to undertake to show that Jefferson was antiquated or unworthy of serious attention on the great question. Calhoun was still a politician and he knew full well the value of a great name.

When Van Buren came to the presidency in 1837, it was not by the votes of the West, nor even of Tennessee, but of the East, New York, Pennsylvania and Virginia, in the main; Van Buren, though the political child of Old Hickory, was a conservative; he understood better than Jackson the meaning of property and a fixed social order. Calhoun saw this and though he hated the New York "magician" he extended him a helping hand against Clay and Webster and sought to secure the support of the administration for the Democratic nomination in 1844.

Having been shipwrecked as a presidential candidate in 1831, he had turned to South Carolina to "rebuild his fences" and hold the state back from its headlong course on the road to secession. In this he succeeded and after banishing from the community irreconcilables like William Smith and Randall Hunt, he became easily the one great figure—the personification of the hotspur state.

JOHN C. CALHOUN

Regarding the tariff as a settled question, he turned in 1837 to the greater problem of negro slavery. The people of his state had never pronounced "the institution" an evil; there were men in Charleston who wrote pamphlets as early as 1803, defending it as a moral and religious arrangement. In Georgia the prevalent idea was that the African slave trade ought not to have been anathematized as piracy in 1819.[1] Now that Alabama and Mississippi were requiring slaves in ever-increasing numbers, Virginia had repented of her earlier heresy and the business of raising negroes for the southern market was not frowned upon.[2]

Calhoun saw the full possibilities of the new situation. He would unite the whole South as he had already united the people of South Carolina. He once said that he would rather have the vote of Virginia than that of all the other

[1] Ames, H. V., *State Documents on Federal Relations,* for reprint of Gov. Troup's Messages on the subject, 1825.

[2] Gov. W. B. Giles in his collection of essays, documents published in 1829; Dew's book already referred to and many pamphlets published in 1832-1833 show this conclusively.

Southern states. What he meant was, that if Virginia and South Carolina came into close affiliation in party and national politics, the other Southern states would soon follow, and it can hardly be doubted that if the Virginia Democrats had rallied to him in 1843 he would have reached the White House in 1845.

The aim then of Calhoun after 1837, when the "old hero" retired, was to conciliate the Jackson men, the people of the growing Northwest, to win the approval of Van Buren and to reach the great goal. Van Buren dallied for a while with the great Nullifier; but the panicky times continued so far into the presidential quadrennium and Thomas Ritchie, editor of the Richmond *Enquirer,* who usually held the Democratic scepter in the Old Dominion, was so timid about Calhoun's chances that no progress could be made with the premature "boom."

The election of 1840 was a reaction in favor of the West and of the Jackson régime, though the Whigs had been the engineers of the movement. The West rose up in its might and struck down the man whom "the money kings" of the East had put into the presidency. Tennessee and Kentucky and every other Mississippi valley state but one, gave great majorities to William Henry Harrison, the man who drank hard cider and wore a coonskin cap. Calhoun delivered the vote of his little state to the "arch-conspirator," Van Buren, and the Old Dominion stood fast by her Democratic guns—a result which augured well for Calhoun's plan of securing the nomination from the party of Old Hickory in 1844.

The little, but growing, circle of the devotees of the South Carolinian realized before the vote was counted in the Senate in 1841 that he was the "logical candidate" of the South and the South would surely name the choice of the party. The new president was not a man of promise, he was inexperienced in the great American game and besides he was an old man who could not— unless he turned out, like Jackson, to grow younger with the increasing weight of responsibility—expect a second term. Clay was the patron of the President and this injured rather than aided him. From 1841 to 1843 the little South Carolina party waged a campaign for the

Democratic nomination in 1844 which Calhoun himself directed and for which he wrote a biography of himself, published and sold, however, as the work of R. M. T. Hunter. He prepared newspaper editorials which were sent to his friends in the Northwest, and his admirers like Robert Winthrop and Abbott Lawrence of Massachusetts, stood ready to sustain his cause with the ever-necessary funds. He did not think the Whigs could either hold together or retain the "log-cabin" popularity which had been so lavishly bestowed.[1]

It was a pathetic figure which Calhoun presented to his friends and to the well-informed in general; he was probably the cleanest man in public life, he hated the game of politics with its subtleties and its pitfalls and he had sworn to himself that if ever he came to power he would apply the axe to the great tree of patronage and affiliated corruption; he knew the workings of the American government better than any of his contemporaries and he appreciated fully the real

[1] Jameson: *Correspondence of John C. Calhoun*, 472, 473-480.

needs of the three great sections of the country and was willing to "give and take" if men would only leave his favorite property, negro slaves, alone. For such a man to be weaving the skein of politics and sowing the seeds of political intrigue, in short, to be compelled to court small politicians and drive hard bargains with the selfish business interests while he himself grew, both consciously and unconsciously, to be a champion of the greatest "interest" of the time, was and still is, a subject of sympathy and interest. I believe that if he had been permitted this time to control the machinery of the party with which he was ready to ally himself and to take the president's chair in 1845, we should have, as historians, to record a different story from that which now occupies our pages, and that both the Texas and the Oregon questions would have been settled peaceably and somewhat to the satisfaction of the angry and contending groups of politicians and their constituents.

But Calhoun had passed the buoyant period of life, and he had done and said so much that politicians like Ritchie and the able intriguer, Robert

J. Walker of Mississippi, Southern men though they were, feared to commit to him the baton of leadership; they thought Calhoun's nomination would surely mean Clay's election, the worst thing, in their minds and Calhoun's, which could possibly happen. He could not win their support and reluctantly he withdrew from the one-sided race and entered Tyler's cabinet only to plan the more industriously for the nomination in 1848. Though Von Holst says that he was simply intriguing for slavery and Texas.

To me this latter seems an untenable view. He had favored annexation but not ardently; the governor of South Carolina as late as November, 1836, had denounced the so-called Texas scheme and George McDuffie can hardly be supposed to have been ill informed as to Calhoun's wishes.[1] Calhoun went into Tyler's cabinet to guide an administration which sorely needed his strong hand and towering reputation and, as has been said, to "shape things" for his own nomination in 1848. That he "pushed" the annexation program which was almost completed when he

[1] Niles *Register*, December 10, 1836.

JOHN C. CALHOUN

took up his portfolio, cannot be doubted; but it proves nothing. What was equally important and more significant as to his own aims and purposes was his prompt overture to Old Hickory through A. J. Donelson. The letter of the great Secretary to Donelson in September, 1844[1] and those of Calhoun's friends like James Gadsden of January, 1844,[2] show that he and they felt that his entry into Tyler's cabinet was to save the Democratic party and to bring about the old alliance between South and West which had promised him so much in 1828. It required even more of sacrifice on his part to invite Jackson's support and coöperation in 1844 than it had to approach Van Buren in 1837, but he was equal to the occasion. Not only did he seek to bring his faction of the party into line with the western faction which Benton fairly represented at that time, but he took such part in the Polk and Dallas campaign as justly to entitle him to much of the honor of the victory which followed. His

[1] Jameson, J. F., *Corresp. of J. C. Calhoun*. Am. Hist. Rep. of '99, II, 614.

[2] Ibid, 916.

ardent South Carolinians he held in check with a steady hand;[1] he sought allies in New England where there was always a very considerable group of Calhoun admirers and he looked steadily to the Northwest where the demand for the annexation of Oregon was almost as strong as that in the South for Texas. His immediate aim was to deliver a final and crushing blow to Clay "[who] had done much to distract the South and to keep the West out of its true position."[2] He was almost certain, as early as September 17, that Clay would be defeated and Polk elected; "it will be the last of Clay" he had said, and the result justified the prophecy.

When the work was done and Polk, "the unknown," came on to Washington for the inauguration, no overture was made to the Carolinian to remain at the national council board, an oversight which was intentional and which Calhoun must have regarded as proof that Jackson had

[1] Jameson, *Corresp.* 616, "The excitement in a portion of Carolina to which you refer has gradually subsided, and will give no further trouble. I had to act with great delicacy, but at the same time firmness in relation to it"; also, ibid, 624.

[2] Jameson, *Corresp.* 617.

resisted his kindly attentions of the preceding autumn, for was not the new president a protégé of Old Hickory and did he not come directly from the Hermitage? But Polk may well have feared to sit down in cabinet meetings with a man who towered above him quite as much as above Tyler and to whom a large element of the South would look as the governor of the country. Gratitude is not a necessary element in the make-up of a public man, certainly it was not to Polk in this case. Calhoun who had done so much to secure Polk his high post and great opportunity was almost snubbed, so curtly was he pushed aside, and the reader of the annals of the time cannot but sympathize with his note to his daughter wherein he says, "it was scarcely in the power of Mr. Polk to treat me badly."[1]

IV

The old hound never hears the horn but he pricks up his ears, and Calhoun on his way home, heard with keen pleasure a toast, offered at a dinner in his honor at Richmond by Ritchie, himself, in which he was addressed as "the next president

[1] Jameson, *Corresp.*, 656.

of the United States."[1] How many times had he not heard words like these in South Carolina and the lower South; but never before from the Virginia king-maker. He was quick to note the incident and to inform his favorite daughter of the changed attitude of Ritchie who was then about to take up his new duties as editor of the Washington *Union,* the administration organ.

The leaders of opinion in the Northwest, men like Douglas of Illinois and the Dodges of Iowa and Wisconsin, had planned a great Mississippi valley convention which was to meet in Memphis in November, 1845. The Southern states and their railway builders were invited to attend. General James Gadsden of South Carolina, Major Tait of Alabama, both railroad presidents, and the industrial leaders generally were interested in the meeting. The Southerners were particularly concerned with expanding their transportation facilities northwestward, while the upper Mississippi states were already looking toward the Pacific. By combining these groups of interests the region which had dominated the country dur-

[1] Ibid, 650.

ing the Jackson "reign" would come again to power; congress could be induced to make land grants to new railroad ventures and the postmaster general would give bonuses for carrying the mails. All this would hasten Western statemaking and permanently fix the power of the proposed Southern-Western alliance. The one great interest of the South, cotton growing, would be advanced and its twin sister, slavery, the more firmly established, for the growing trade between the farmers of the Ohio and the upper Mississippi valleys and the plantations of the South would tie the two sections together.

Under these circumstances it is not surprising that we find Calhoun presiding over the Memphis convention. Indeed so full of the new or, with him, old program and its probable consequences had he become that he surpassed the utmost expectations of the industrial promoters of the West by commending to the convention and to the country, in his carefully prepared address,[1] a return to the era and the idea of internal improvements which he had discarded and denounced a

[1] Crallé, R. K., *Works of Calhoun*, V. 293-311.

dozen years before. To the new railroad ventures within state boundaries he would have the federal government guarantee long term mail contracts at rates above the accustomed price, and free iron for construction purposes which would have amounted to a bonus of $2,000 a mile, while to those within the territories he was not opposed to direct government grants. Canal builders and cities like Chicago and Louisville where good harbor facilities were wanted should receive assistance on the ground that the Mississippi and its tributaries were "inland seas" which might be improved under the powers of the constitution which allowed the harbors of the Atlantic and Gulf coasts to draw large sums from the national strong box. The superficial student of Calhoun's speeches and teachings between 1833 and 1845 may be surprised at this apparent desertion of his national policy; not so with him who reads between the lines and who fully comprehends the purposes and the motives of the man. He is now as always, a nationalist, if only the politicians will allow, but a nationalist who, like most, if not all, other leaders in American public life, demanded

JOHN C. CALHOUN

first protection to his constituents. The first duty of Webster in congress when a young man was to champion the cause of New England free traders who made up the majority of his constituents; but in 1828, when his constituents had become manufacturers, he made quite an able defense of the cause of protection and two years later he was the author of a doctrine of "new nationality" since the nation was the only power which could give protection; and finally when his ambition to be president had become as overpowering as Calhoun's he could make eloquent periods in defense of the Union and of slavery. Calhoun's course was not different: he was a nationalist when South Carolina adhered to the same view, he became a particularist when South Carolina's interests were endangered; he was always a pro-slavery man because both his state and his section were pro-slavery.

But his "defection" at Memphis, his "inland seas" doctrines gave smaller men in the South much trouble; men who see only the small space "before their noses" thought that he had deserted the South, that he was granting the latitudinarian doctrine which would certainly lead to national interference with slavery. Jefferson Davis refused to apologize for or to defend the new idea[1] though he later learned to plan great combinations like that which underlay the Memphis address. Calhoun's followers labored under the blighting inability of not being able to see that twice two make four, and they began their campaign of "doubts and fears" which have so often defeated the larger planning of the larger men of the republic. The administration could not understand Calhoun except that Polk knew that he desired the presidency in 1848; Thomas Ritchie was now, only six months after the Richmond toast, certain that the Democracy would be defeated if it ventured such a program and such a nomination; South Carolina, under the influence of the epigones of nullification, protested that even "the prophet" had gone astray. There was probably never a chance for Calhoun after the break with Jackson, but Calhoun could not so understand the signs of the time. His very virtues were weights

[1] Davis, Mrs. Jefferson, *Memoirs of Jefferson Davis*, 211-213; Dodd, W. E., *Life of Jefferson Davis*, 68.

JOHN C. CALHOUN

about his feet; small men are offended at the very presence of greatness. Besides, Calhoun had permitted himself to be blinded by the love of property rights, not of property, for never was there a less avaricious statesman. He had unconsciously become a representative of the "interests," a reactionary to whom the chief value of the Constitution consisted in its guarantee of property against the aggressions of democracy and the enthusiasm of the younger generation of Americans on behalf of human rights and personal liberty. Returning from his visit to the Southwest, he wrote his daughter that everywhere he went the people flocked to see and hear him. The crowds were even greater than those which had greeted the "General" on his last tour and this seemed to give him much comfort.[1] When he reached South Carolina it was generally understood that he had retired to his plantation at Fort Hill in the beautiful up-country region to await the call of his party to enter upon the presidential canvass as standard-bearer in 1848.

But the coming war with Mexico was the talk

[1] Jameson, *Corresp.* 674.

154 STATESMEN OF THE OLD SOUTH

everywhere, and Polk, in his first annual message, seemed to court a conflict with England as well. In other words, Polk took the recent platform of his party calling for "all Texas and all Oregon" seriously. He was a simple, honest man who believed in the creed he professed. Calhoun was astounded at such simplicity; he had thought the preëlection talk was intended only to win votes. Not only had the President come out for "all Oregon or fight" but congress began its deliberations with resolutions to give England notice of the American intentions which Calhoun said would surely bring war.[1]

Feeling that the country was at the threshold of a great crisis, he indicated, and he had only to indicate, that he would accept another term in the United States Senate. On his way to Washington, the London *Times* hailed him as the friend of peace and the New York *Journal of Commerce* thought he would be the savior of his country. The head of Tammany Hall wrote that "J. C. Calhoun needs but to stand still and as sure as the day comes, so sure will '49 see him where his

[1] Ibid, 674.

deserts long since should have placed him."[1] Even the American minister to England wrote him in detail about the state of politics there in order that he might save the country in spite of the President. Calhoun's friends were sounding public opinion everywhere and informing him daily that he would certainly be the next president, though one group of them urged him to stand with Polk and for the war, while the other urged the "masterly inactivity" which should win without war both Texas and Oregon. The latter gained his ear, and his attitude[2] was fixed. If ever Calhoun had reason to think himself infallible, it was at this time when all the world was pronouncing him the great statesman, the great Calhoun! It was the last time in his long career that he saw the highest prize in America glittering before him.

Calhoun stood with the South on the Oregon question, i. e. he was a moderate. His position was a deciding factor in the compromise which fixed the boundary at the 49th parallel and he

[1] Letter of Fernando Wood in Jameson, *Corresp.* 1065-67.

[2] Jameson, *Corresp.*, 1058-60.

received the thanks of conservative men in all sections regardless of party affiliations.[1] He thought that he had prevented war with England and there is much reason to agree with him. In this he received the hearty endorsement of most people of the South, too, where a war on behalf of the far-off Oregon country was certainly not desired. But when the administration forced hostilities with Mexico he denounced the President's program and declared that Polk did not desire a peaceful solution of the Texas problem. In fact, he saw early what direction the leaders of the party were taking, namely, national aggrandizement at the expense of Mexico, and he foretold the ruin that such a policy would bring upon the slavery interest whose champions were headlong leaders of what may properly be called the imperialistic wing of the Democratic party. All of Mexico, not all of Oregon, is what men like Jefferson Davis desired; and two years had not passed before they were planning a Panama canal, an expanding commerce

---

[1] A fair illustration is the letter of Edward Everett, Jameson, *Corresp.* 1080-81.

JOHN C. CALHOUN

with the Orient, and talking of the absorption of the ill-governed land of the Montezumas—"an ocean-bound republic" was their cry. It was the swelling ambition of the lower South which Polk allowed to prevail and which men like Lewis Cass and Senator Allen of Ohio were only too glad to encourage in the hope that they might succeed to the post which was to be denied Calhoun.

After a year of war, the administration became uneasy about compelling Mexico to cede New Mexico and California in time to face the next general election with the best of all arguments, success, and the military committee of the Senate headed by Cass brought in the plan which became known to the country as the "Ten Regiments" bill. Cass asked for ten thousand regulars and thirty millions of dollars with which to accomplish the task. The growing purpose of Robert J. Walker, Secretary of the Treasury, Jefferson Davis and others, was to take over all Mexico,[1] though this was not openly declared in the Senate discussions. Viewing the whole Southern program now with alarm, Calhoun threw the weight

[1] Bourne, E. G., *American Historical Review*, V, 491.

of his influence against the scheme and defeated it. The Southern imperialists could not understand him; they were angry, but could not safely show it. Was not the South to be the chief beneficiary of annexation and was not Calhoun the very incarnation of Southern purpose and ambition? Calhoun had been courted by the President,[1] urged by the war party and stimulated by the promise of support for his campaign for the Democratic nomination in 1848. It availed nothing; he not only spoke against the measure but called attention of the country to the dangerous policy[2] of the Polk administration.

While his slender chances for the nomination had been thus thrown away during the sessions of 1845-46 and 1846-47, the Wilmot proviso, a "rider" attached to the Two Million bill of 1846, forever forbidding slavery in the territory about to be acquired from Mexico, became the burning issue. Wilmot was a weak unimportant member of the House, but he presented a test question which set the groups in the Democratic party by

[1] *The Polk Diary*, II, 282—on.

[2] *Works*, IV, 303-327, for speech in full.

JOHN C. CALHOUN 159

the ears in a way which augured ill for both the dominant party and for the country. Cass, who was playing fast and loose for the succession and who had the best claims on the imperialist wing of his party, at first supported the proviso which he later pronounced unconstitutional; Benton who felt that the whole Texas-Oregon policy was his "thunder" and that it had been stolen by the Southerners at Baltimore, was disposed to favor the idea if for no other purpose than to injure Calhoun whose schemes for the support of the Northwest were already giving him trouble in Missouri; the President thought the move only the blunder of an innocent member of congress, whom he sent for and persuaded to recede from his position.[1] But to Calhoun it was a challenge which he took up at once and which threw him and all his followers into hysteria. He watched the moves of the "Wilmot men" and the growing favor they received in the Northwest during the session of congress which closed in March, 1847. And when he returned to South Carolina he was greeted by an immense throng of people

[1] *Polk's Diary*, II, 289.

who regarded the Wilmot restriction as a declaration of war against slavery and the South. In an address which he delivered in Charleston on March 9, 1847,[1] he returned to his radical particularism of 1832. Any interference with slavery in any of the territories should be prohibited by congress whose business it was to protect property, and negro slaves were nothing else. If congress refused the protection which the Constitution promised, the South must defend herself. This is in brief the idea which went out to the country from Charleston. Southern papers reprinted his words as coming from a seer; both Whig and Democratic journals vied with each other in the race to radicalism on this subject— a radicalism on behalf of property rights, a reaction from those nobler ideas of the South which had given Jefferson his fame and which in a way animated Jackson. Virginia declared in her legislature of the ensuing autumn that she would go to war rather than see the Wilmot proviso become law. The people of Mississippi assembled in mass meetings, and regardless of party align-

[1] Jameson, *Corresp.*, 719; *Works* IV, 382.

ments, took steps toward secession. South Carolina, under the same leadership which had produced the nullification movement fifteen years before, rode upon the crest of the new storm. Thus far was loyalty to property ideals carrying a noble people and one of the ablest leaders the nation has ever produced. Calhoun, the nationalist, who had less than two years before planned at Memphis with the Chicago business men and the northwestern politicians a movement like that which had made him a great figure in 1816, was now falling back behind his second line of defense—slavery and the monopoly rights which its protagonists enjoyed. From 1847 to the day of his death in 1850, he strove as he had never striven before to unite the people of the South on the one issue upon which unity was ominous.

The treaty with Mexico which fixed the status in the union of California, New Mexico, and Texas, was a sort of title deed which Polk labored so long and faithfully to present to the country at the close of his administration. The country accepted the gift with thanks but repudiated the giver. Neither Polk nor any other member of

162 STATESMEN OF THE OLD SOUTH

his party possessed the confidence of the nation in a sufficient degree to secure the presidency. Calhoun, who had warned the imperialists, had now no hope for high promotion, and he gave all his strength to the task of winning and holding the new areas for the South and for slavery although he had confessed to Polk in 1846[1] that slavery could never be maintained in the new region. What he contended for was the shadow of a victory just as the Wilmot proviso men were doing, both parties acknowledging that it was a victory, not practical results, which they had in view, a fact which Webster might have offered in justification of his famous debacle of March 7, 1850.

It was to Calhoun a most painful situation, but one for which he was more responsible than any other man. He marshalled his forces for the conflict like the great general he was. Jefferson Davis and James M. Mason were his lieutenants in the Senate while Robert Barnwell Rhett and William Lowndes Yancey surpassed themselves in arousing the South to the dangers which seemed to threaten the two billions of dollars

[1] *Polk's Diary,* II, 283-84.

worth of negro property scattered all the way from Pennsylvania to the Rio Grande. It is not worth while to describe here the scenes which have been depicted so often: how the South was assembling in a sort of second Hartford convention at Nashville, how the leading Southern senators and representatives held meetings and caucuses from day to day, how Calhoun warned the Southern people in a formal address[1] that their dearest rights were at stake. It was an exciting time, calling for the coolest heads; Calhoun was already in his sixty-eighth year and possessed now, as always, of a cool head and calculating mind. Still he led the revolt. Calhoun, unlike most other men, was as "high strung," as ambitious and as keen a debater the last year of his life as when he first entered congress. But it was the South, not the young and struggling nation of 1811 for which he strove so manfully and sadly in 1850. He did not live to see the surrender of his followers to the genius of his life-long rival, Clay, who had come back to congress to wrestle with him.

[1] *Works.* VI 285-312.

When Calhoun died, March 31, 1850, literally at his post in Washington, there was little sign that Southern men, like Foote of Mississippi, would "go over" to Clay or that the sunshine of the great orator's diffusive personality would dissolve the bellicose Southern convention; and well might one say of Calhoun as of Washington, he died at the right time, being spared the bitter cup preparing for him, though it required the death of a younger and more vigorous man than Calhoun, none less than President Taylor himself, to secure the desired end, the third and last great compromise of the Kentucky statesman.

It was a black day for the people of the Palmetto state that brought the news of Calhoun's death. Men put on the signs of mourning and women wept as they went about their domestic duties. "The great Calhoun is dead" was the low murmur which passed from house to house and town to town throughout the devoted little state. Merchant princes of Charleston, plantation masters of the cotton belt, simple farmers from the up-country wore the badge of genuine grief. So long had the dead senator lived and moved among his people, so long had they looked to him as a divine oracle in times of stress that men knew not what to do now that he was gone. Calhoun was the state of South Carolina and the state of South Carolina was quite as sacred to its people as was ever Stuart or Bourbon prince to his followers. For a whole month the remains of the departed statesman were kept above ground in order that the living might have a chance to show their respect, and when the tomb claimed its own, the people still lingered about the sacred spot like those who mourn their departed mates. And when the war came ten years later his remains were brought to Charleston and kept under a guard of two companies of South Carolina troops lest by some chance the hostile North should get opportunity to wreak its vengeance upon his mouldering frame. Calhoun still lived; and he lives to-day in a sense that no other American leader lives. His memory is worshiped by tens of thousands; even the poor negroes sing his praises and tell stories of his unmatched greatness.

It was not Jefferson's lot to embody either during his life or after his death the thought and feelings of a whole state or any considerable part of the nation; the "Sage of Monticello" was ever a partisan and men of wealth even in the capital of the Old Dominion, revile both his name and his teachings to this day. Men remember Jefferson's ideas and ideals, not his personality, and they still contend for and dispute about them. No man doubts what Calhoun stood for; and the people of the South know well that it was he who prepared the way for secession and war. The author has heard small cotton farmers declaim how the South would have won but for his death ten years before the war.

He had begun, the son of a small planter, whose father had been an anti-slavery man, had become a slaveholder through no fault of his own, married a lady of the aristocratic régime in Charleston and turned his attention to national politics. He became at once an ardent nationalist, impelled onward by the sectionalism of New England, and was one of the great figures of that period of reconstruction which followed the second war with England. Compelled by the injustice and bad faith of a personal and despotic party leader, he turned his matchless genius to the invention of a doctrine which should reconcile nationality with particularism, and became at once the champion of slavery and cotton, the money interests of the South. From 1833 to 1850 he taught the South that property in negro slaves was more sacred than the rights and ideas so eloquently defended by his own great teacher, Jefferson. He died, the greatest reactionary of his time.

War was to be the next stage in the evolution, and Jefferson Davis was to complete the work of Calhoun and convert the old and radical democracy of Jefferson into armies contending upon the field of battle for ideals and purposes absolutely foreign to the mind of the great founder.

FROM RADICALISM TO CONSERVATIVE REVOLT

JEFFERSON DAVIS

I

TO speak kindly of Jefferson Davis, even a half-century after the events which he helped to bring about, is an exceedingly risky thing. Somehow or other, mankind requires scapegoats; somebody must be punished for the mistakes of the race or the nation, and no better way has been found than to pick out some conspicuous individual, usually innocent and sometimes even harmless, and lay upon him the burden of shame and guilt for great calamities which have come as a result of the general sinning. I shall not here and now enter upon a defense of this system nor even of the innocent victims of it in history, but only remark that we have adopted the system in America, that we like it and that there is no telling when some of us may be pounced upon by our community or our country as a scapegoat. Jefferson Davis was a scapegoat and he bore upon himself the marks of the general disapproval until he was laid to rest in his tomb in romantic Hollywood cemetery on the banks of the James. Keeping this idea in mind I think we may profitably study the remarkable career of the man who headed the greatest revolt in human history and whose work came nearer to success than that of any other who finally failed.

Jefferson Davis was like Lincoln, born on the Kentucky frontier—in the Green river valley, whence his parents had gone from Georgia in search of a better station in life and some lands for their tribe of children. Pioneers, especially Kentucky pioneers, seem to have won the special approval of Providence if Providence approves of large families. Henry Clay's mother gave seventeen sons and daughters to old Kentucky—there was a clan of Clays; Chief Justice Marshall's father carried thirteen children to his new home in the West and Samuel Davis, though not blessed so frequently, was the father of nine sons and

JEFFERSON DAVIS

daughters, of whom Jefferson was the youngest.

With so great a household it was a problem indeed for the Davises to find sustenance, and the father like Lincoln's father was restless. He did not remain a long time in Kentucky; but on hearing of the great wealth to be made in the new cotton planting industry, embarked his household goods upon the Mississippi in 1810, two years after young Jefferson's advent into the world, and took up lands in the new Louisiana territory. Discontented still, he moved next year to the southwestern border of Mississippi where he found lands and conditions to suit his needs about fifty miles from the then thriving town of Natchez.

The Davises, it will be noticed, were, like the Jeffersons and the Calhouns, borderers—men who live and bring up their families on the outskirts of civilization and who accustom themselves to the absence of most of those accessories of life which most of us regard as essential. There was not much comfort in the home of young Thomas Jefferson and he saw a rough life of it, with Indians taking scalps now and then in his neighborhood; as we have seen, John Calhoun knew what it meant to lose his nearest of kin by Indian warfare; and young Jefferson Davis was hardly out of his cradle before Calhoun's war of 1812 turned loose the southern Indians to wreak their vengeance upon the innocent and the guilty alike.

There was another similarity in the situation of Davis to that of Calhoun and Jefferson—he was a child of the new West of his day. The first counties established in Mississippi were Wilkinson, Amite and Adams—names which young Davis first learned to pronounce. Not only on the border, but as an exponent of a new West, he came to man's estate and to leadership in the affairs of the South. The Davis family was "Hardshell" Baptist as the ugly term now goes—proof enough that he was "rocked" in the same kind of a cradle that "rocked" young Lincoln whose father had taken him off to the border forests of Indiana and Illinois. The local schoolmaster in Davis' neighborhood was one Shaw, who gathered the boys of the community into a little log schoolhouse to teach them the mysteries of the three R's. But as fate will have it, the teacher was an uncommon good one, an émigré from Boston, like Jefferson's and Calhoun's teachers, representatives of learning in a far country doing missionary work—great work as their pupils' lives made fully evident in the days to come.

But Jefferson's West grew strong in opposing the royal governors of Virginia; Calhoun's in fighting the Federalist reaction and the Charleston clique; while the West of Jefferson Davis was a cotton growing section which looked upon the federal government, like the protectionists of the East, as an agency whose primary business it was to foster and protect industry. Human rights as such, theories of government and the growth of a great homogeneous nationality such as Jefferson and Calhoun struggled to attain, were far from the minds of these pioneers of the lower South. Still it was a wholesome, democratic community aside from the one great interest—cotton planting and slavery, its concomitant.

When young Davis was ready for college, he was sent to the so-called Athens of the West,

Lexington, Kentucky, where a Connecticut teacher had built one of the greatest colleges in the country, judged by the number of students present and the variety of subjects offered. Transylvania University was indeed a great institution when Holley was at its head and when Speaker Henry Clay was its patron. Ambitious students from all the states and territories west of the Alleghanies flocked there to procure the necessary training for public careers. Jefferson advised young Virginians to repair to the Kentucky fountain of learning as the source of true republicanism. In support of the college Lexington established the first public library in the West and both town and state boasted of "the University" in a way that should have compelled a greater success than has since been accorded to it. Latin and Greek and Mathematics were the three R's of Davis' collegiate training and he pursued them with a fair degree of diligence considering his strong bent for other things. Davis was not the boy to break down his health with hard study as Calhoun had been nor to "push" himself like Jefferson into the society of his teachers in order to listen to their "sweet discourse of books." Davis did not "graduate," as Americans insist upon saying when a young man completes his four years' course at college. He liked to tease his professors and play pranks upon the unoffending, if somewhat inviting, citizens of the town and he enjoyed living and breathing the fresh outdoor, Kentucky atmosphere, all of which was contrary to the law of the place and the wishes of his superiors—traits which college boys elsewhere have sometimes developed.

From Transylvania Davis was sent to West Point where he met Robert E. Lee and Albert Sidney Johnston, men who became famous co-workers of his in the great struggle for Southern independence. At the National Military Academy he received the training which he most desired and though he did not win a high stand in his class, he seems to have imbibed the spirit of the place as thoroughly as any who ever entered upon its courses. Davis was all his life a "military man" with the military air and some of the class consciousness which many other West Pointers have shown in abundance. The simple democratic boy who "went off to college" in 1821 came home in 1828 "every inch" an aristocrat, which was probably what Joseph Davis, the oldest brother, and head of the family since the father's death in 1828, desired, for the fortunes of the Davises had greatly improved. Joseph Davis was fast becoming a millionaire and a great planter who felt a keen interest in the young army officer whose fortune already promised so much.

The five or six years which young Davis now spent on the northwestern frontier did not materially change his views of life or his already fixed character. His marriage to the daughter of Colonel Zachary Taylor at the close of his army service in 1835 was more important in drawing out the character of the man than in seriously affecting his destiny. It was clandestine. The Taylor homestead was then on the Ohio near Louisville, Kentucky; but Taylor and his daughter lived at old Fort Crawford in southwestern Wisconsin. In order to get rid of an ambitious suitor for the hand of the young lady, Taylor sent the young lieutenant to Fort Gibson in Arkansas, some four hundred miles away. As usual locks and keys proved of no avail against the desires of the young lovers. Miss Taylor made a visit to her father's sister who lived in a small frame house on the banks of the Ohio about five miles from the older Taylor estate. Davis visited the place at the same time, despite the distance of nearly a thousand miles and carried off the prize to his brother's great plantation, Hurricane, on the Mississippi, a little below Vicksburg.

Here in the year 1835 Davis began the career of a cotton planter, so profitable in the thirties and fifties of the last century. He bought negroes "on credit," and built a small plantation house on the land which his brother gave him as his part of the deceased father's estate. Working with his own hands among his negroes in the cotton fields was in his case, as in Calhoun's, not inconsistent with the ideals of the Southern people, though the great planters were seldom seen on their plantations except on horseback, giving orders to overseers. In a few months both Davis and his wife were stricken by the fever which attacks the unacclimated in the hot delta region.

The young wife died, but the husband slowly recovered, not regaining his strength until a year later. Davis never enjoyed vigorous health after the terrible experiences of his service as an army officer in the northwest corner of Wisconsin in 1828-30, and neither as a planter nor as United States senator nor yet as president of the Confederacy did he ever for any considerable period count himself a "well" man. He often arose from a sick bed to make his speeches in the Senate; the orders for the assembling of the Confederate troops at Manassas in 1861 were issued while he lay prostrate in his private chamber, and when he retired to Mississippi after two years' imprisonment he was of course a "physical wreck," though the spirit of the man was still equal to many a storm. Jefferson Davis is a perfect example of what a resolute will can endure and accomplish in spite of the most depressing and incurable of maladies.

Eight years, beginning with 1837, were next spent on the plantation at Davis Bend, Warren county, Mississippi, and aside from the work of the plantation Davis read history, both ancient and contemporary, as few Southerners of his day were doing and when he emerged in 1843 as a candidate for election to the state legislature as a Democrat from a Whig constituency, he was ready even for the debate with the great orator Sergeant Prentiss, which was forced upon him. It was a better discussion, we are told, than that which occurred in Virginia between young John Randolph and the aged Patrick Henry in 1798. The debate and the candidacy made one thing clear if nothing else, that the future Confederate chieftain never defended but opposed the then widely discussed policy of repudiation advocated by his party. But Davis was defeated in his first ambition, though the reputation which he won pointed him out to the "boss" of the state, Robert J. Walker, as presidential elector in 1844, when the slender, angular form of Jefferson Davis first became known to the people of every county in Mississippi. He had the satisfaction of voting for the successful candidate of that momentous campaign and a year later he was sent on to congress "to win his spurs" in national politics, i.e., in December, 1845, the year when Calhoun, his great mentor, was planning his last hopeless campaign for the presidency.

Davis was already known as a follower of Calhoun in much the same way that Calhoun had been counted a disciple of Jefferson in 1810; but in the one case as in the other there was too much independence for either simply to tread "beaten paths." Davis was essentially an aristocrat; Calhoun had been a democrat as was Jefferson before him, though both the Virginian and the Carolina leader were aristocrats in personal tastes and feelings. Davis, though a Democrat in politics, was a representative of the "interests" of the lower South; Jefferson had been in 1776, and always remained, an enemy of the "interests" both in Virginia and in the nation; thus we see the metamorphosis of the old Republican party in the positions of its representative men. But Davis was not yet the Voice of the lower South or of his state.

Mississippi was in 1844 the aggressive Southern state; it was the South Carolina of 1812. The leaders of Mississippi when Davis entered public life had just displaced the Tennessee group which had but recently passed its zenith, though the Mississippians picked a Tennesseean for president. No wiser politician ever had a seat in the United States Senate than Robert J. Walker of Pennsylvania-Mississippi, senator since 1836, master planner of the Baltimore Democratic convention which "slaughtered" Van Buren and showed Calhoun how futile had been all his efforts to attain the nomination for the presidency and who at the right time introduced Polk and carried off the honors. No better piece of "wire-pulling" was ever done by the late Mark Hanna than that which culminated in the nomination of Polk and Dallas—the one a low tariff man to please Calhoun, the other a protectionist to win Pennsylvania and, in order to hold the Northwest to the lower South, "fifty-four forty or fight" (for Oregon) was added, in the platform, to the Mississippi slogan, the "reannexation of Texas." What proved the wisdom of Walker was the election which showed every Southern state but three, North Carolina, Tennessee and Kentucky, and every Northwestern state but one, Ohio, "solid" for Polk and Dallas.

What Calhoun had planned for all his life and failed to accomplish was thus won by the Mississippi senator in a campaign of less than a year! The South and the West had united fortunes once more as in 1800 and in 1828.

Walker's co-workers in Mississippi were John A. Quitman, a New Yorker, Jacob Thompson, a North Carolinian, Alexander G. Brown, a South Carolinian, Henry S. Foote, a Virginian, and Jefferson Davis, a Kentuckian. None of these men were planters native to Mississippi, some were former Jackson men, some ardent supporters of Calhoun, but all had done men's work and more in electing Polk. What they asked for in national politics was what they obtained, the annexation of Texas. What was to come after—war with Mexico, expansion to the Pacific and a new crisis about slavery—was not a matter that gave them any great concern. The rapid rise in the value of negro property, like stocks on Wall street when new regions of exploitation offer, was a perfectly natural consequence of the Mississippi policies. The annexation of Louisiana had produced a similar result in 1803; and in 1855

JEFFERSON DAVIS

Henry A. Wise, of Virginia, declared to his people that the making of Kansas a slave state would "raise the price of your negroes" a hundred per cent.

Walker became Polk's secretary of treasury and dominated to a large degree the whole administration; John A. Quitman and Jefferson Davis became brigadier-generals in the Mexican war; A. G. Brown was governor of Mississippi; Jacob Thompson remained in the House; and Henry S. Foote went to the United States Senate. Was ever a small group of leaders—all living in a small and new state—more successful or more influential?

Davis was the youngest member of the Mississippi coterie. Walker was its master and mouthpiece. A small wizen-faced, stooping figure, unattractive and unprepossessing to a high degree, he was, nevertheless, the architect of the democratic imperialism under which Texas was annexed, and New Mexico and California were taken as a recompense for not taking Texas earlier. The only difference between Walker's view and the policy of the federal government as it was finally carried out was that he demanded all Mexico to save future troubles and excuses about Panama and the canal.

Davis was heart and soul with his Mississippi patron and when he came back from Mexico with the honors of Buena Vista "thick upon him," Governor Brown appointed him to the then vacant seat for Mississippi in the United States Senate. "General" Davis, young though he was and a new member of the "most august legislative body on earth," took rank at once with the first in the land. Calhoun had come back to "die in the last ditch;" Webster was there, too; and Benton and Lewis Cass, the latter soon to be the defeated candidate of his party for the presidency, were leaders. Placed on the committee on military affairs, of which Cass was chairman, Davis had opportunity to work out a policy for himself, his committee, and the country, for this was just then the most important committee in congress. The plan was simple: send forward to the scene of war ten new regiments of regular troops, well supported by the militia forces already in the service, hold all Mexico and never give up the southern part of the country if any. The coun-

JEFFERSON DAVIS

try is ours by right of conquest—a right which few nations will dare dispute. The obliteration of Mexico or its restoration was a matter for Congress to decide, not for the newspapers, least of all for the Mexicans who had appealed to the last argument of nations and had lost.

Though an ardent admirer of Calhoun, Davis had no patience with his program, which was the one finally adopted; viz., the restoration of Mexico and the cession to the United States of New Mexico and California. The older man, foreseeing what an awful struggle would ensue over the question of slavery in the proposed enormous accessions, preferred the more moderate course; the younger flushed with victory and just beginning his career as a national leader, was willing to take the risk and appeal to the country to return the party to power in 1848. It need not be said that the Calhoun policy was the wiser both for the nation and for the lower South, then dominant in the nation.

The people in the election which followed repudiated the party which had settled the Texas and Oregon questions and annexed territory sufficient to make a dozen states. They went further and indicated, though not very clearly, that they did not intend that slavery should be extended over the new territories. The South, which four years before had won a great triumph and apparently consummated the alliance with the West, was now threatened with the loss of the reins of government and of all the benefits of the recent war. The only consoling feature of the late campaign was that the president-elect was a great slaveholder and might in the end be relied on to see that no harm befell "the institution." From Davis's point of view the failure of the South to support Cass was fatal, though Taylor was, it will be recalled, the father of his first wife and his commander at Buena Vista. His idea was that the West which was "solid" for Cass should be solidly supported by the South and that the alliance of the two sections would not only guarantee the country against the dangers of the abolitionists but secure the interests of the South. Cass was not unwilling that slavery should go into the territories, in fact, after some wavering, he was able to find a constitutional mandate in favor of slavery in the disputed region. Davis made speeches in Louisiana and Mississippi against his father-in-law, yet everywhere declaring the general to be both a noble man and a great soldier and, in consequence of this moderation and of his relationship to the president, it was expected in Washington in March, 1849, that the Mississippi senator would have great influence at the White House during the incoming administration.

But when the new president came out for the admission of California as a free state, not only Davis, but the South in general, was bitterly disappointed. Furthermore, the president threatened to send the United States army into New Mexico if the people who were trying to make that region pro-slavery did not desist. The crisis of 1850 had been foreshadowed by the election of 1848; its bitterness was assured by the determined attitude of the new administration. Davis and Foote left Mississippi in November, 1849, convinced that the people of that state would secede rather than allow the admission of California as a free state. There was almost unanimity of feeling on the subject. Whigs were disgusted with

Taylor, and Democrats were enraged. The mass meetings which assembled in various places not only in Mississippi but in the South as a whole were attended by the leaders of both parties. And these meetings called for a general Southern convention to take counsel what to do in the coming conflict. Davis was convinced that the South should demand the extension of the line of 36° 30′ to the Pacific and that new states south of that line should be admitted as slave states and that southern California should of course come in at once as a slave state.

There is no space in a paper like this to discuss the long debates in congress, the Nashville convention and the final submission of the South to the compromise legislation of 1850. Davis thought that the South should have stood together to the last and that Southern states should have taken steps toward secession when their ultimatum as to California was not heeded. He believed, and I think he was correct in this, that Clay and Fillmore, after the death of Taylor in 1850, would have yielded all that was asked. What brought the humiliation of the South was in his opinion, the demagoguery of Alexander Stephens, his own colleague, Henry S. Foote, and the weakness of John Bell of Tennessee. When Foote declared in the Senate that Davis no longer represented the public opinion of Mississippi, the latter, unlike the present habit of senators, offered to resign and challenged his colleague to do the same and go home and fight it out before the people. Foote accepted. They became rival candidates for the governorship of the state and canvassed the counties of Mississippi much after the fashion of Douglas and Lincoln in 1858. The decision was in favor of Foote, and Davis retired to his estate a stranded politician with little prospect of ever emerging again as a leader and exponent of his state. It would be interesting indeed to read his private correspondence during the years 1851 and 1852, but this seems to be impossible since most of his papers and library were destroyed by federal troops in 1863 during the Vicksburg campaign. But I believe Davis gave up the idea of secession and the hope of united action on the part of the Southern states.

II

In this case as in many another the unexpected happened. The Democrats won in the election of 1852 and Davis, the former extremist, was selected for a principal place in the new cabinet. Pierce owed neither his nomination nor his election to Davis; in fact, Mississippi leaders had less to do with this campaign than almost any other Southern group. But Franklin Pierce was a personal friend of Davis, and Caleb Cushing of Massachusetts, who was a still closer friend, was also very close to the president-elect. Cushing and Pierce talked over Southern men and Davis was their choice. No abler man could have been selected from the South, though it is very doubtful if he would have been chosen by the voters of that section as a representative. It may as well be said now as later that his administration of the war department was regarded as peculiarly able and satisfactory to all groups of opinion in the country, and the old story that he used his office to prepare the way for secession is utterly unworthy of credence in the light of the facts and of his own history.

JEFFERSON DAVIS

Pierce had won the electoral votes of every state in the Union except four: Massachusetts, Vermont, Kentucky and Tennessee, and this overwhelming victory was due to the feeling of the country that there had been agitation enough and that slavery, definitely limited to a certain area, was not henceforth to be the bone of contention between the North and the South. I cannot say from documentary evidence that Davis was also of this opinion, but it seems to me that such was undoubtedly his view.

What sort of man was this Davis, destined, as it turned out, to be the backbone of the administrations of both Pierce and Buchanan? He was a tall, spare man forty-four years old, with large gray eyes, rather large and irregular features; his limbs were long and slender and rather loosely joined together, reminding one of his fellow Kentuckian whose fame was so soon to fill the earth, Abraham Lincoln. He was full six feet tall and carried himself well, as do most "West Pointers"; every inch an aristocrat, as Carl Schurz, who saw him about this time, said. He seldom walked about Washington during his eight years residence there just preceding the civil war; but everybody knew him and almost every one liked him. His carriage took him daily to his office or to the President's house where he was welcome at all times; or in the afternoon he might have been seen on a handsome saddle horse going out to Cabin John's Bridge or watching the progress of the work on the present capitol which was completed under his supervision. Strength, will, imperious determination sat upon the brow and countenance of this man of feeble health but iron constitution.

During the four years that Davis was at the head of the war department, he formulated both for the President and himself the policy which he was to follow until 1861 and which but for Stephen A. Douglas would in all probability have become the settled policy of the country. This was the building of a Southern Pacific railway with its eastern terminus at Memphis, the acquisition of the Panama canal zone, the purchase of Cuba, the opening of Japan and China to American trade, and the cultivation of closer commercial relations with South America. This was a bold scheme, but it cannot be said that it was very different from that which has been actually followed by the country from that day until the present time. There was something, too, in the program for all sections and interests, though the South was to have the lion's share just as the North has given herself under post-bellum administrations. Undoubtedly Caleb Cushing, one of the very greatest minds Massachusetts has ever produced—though one does not hear this in Boston—was in part the author of this program, and the President was entitled to call it "my policies."

Davis, the former strict constructionist and follower of Calhoun, the arch-secessionist, announced a part of the general plan, his rôle in particular, the Pacific railway, to a Philadelphia audience in the autumn of 1853. It was astonishing, yet the "captains of industry" liked it and Southern leaders were pleased if only it could be carried without raising that everlasting question, constitutionality. Davis arranged this point nicely by proposing to build the road under the war powers of the federal government. That sounds like Calhoun in the early days when he was war secretary or like Clay when he was planning his first great American highway, or not unlike Calhoun's notable Memphis program of 1845. And the idea was based on the same general scheme of politics: the alliance of the South and West—the old theme of Jefferson in 1800, of Calhoun and Clay in 1812 and of Jackson in 1828. How many times has not this plan filled the mind of politician and statesman in this country! And now that Pierce had practically all the country behind him, why not? Certainly there was enough in the scheme to make a president and Davis was not averse to the hum of that famous bee, though his ambition was not hasty, nor his electioneering evident. He proposed to build the road and then seek the presidency or at any rate make a good beginning. One thing he miscalculated, the capacity of the people of the Northwest for self-sacrifice, for his scheme involved, to a certain extent, the isolation of the middle and northwestern states. It would have made St. Louis a Chicago and Memphis a St. Louis.

Many men in Illinois saw the meaning of the

Davis plan; but that might not have meant so much had it not been for their leader, Stephen A. Douglas, whose love for the Middle West was quite as great as that of Davis for the South. Douglas returned to his place in the Senate in December following the Philadelphia utterance with a plan of his own—one which would satisfy Chicago interests and give new lands to the restless Iowa pioneer.

Senator Douglas had been a strong competitor of Pierce for the nomination in 1852, but Douglas was not invited to become a member of the cabinet as might have been expected. The representatives of the West in the Pierce cabinet were James Guthrie, a railroad president from Kentucky, and Robert McClellan, a Michigan politician, whose name counted for nothing in national affairs. In the West there were two interests contending for the supremacy: that of the St. Louis railway promoters headed by Benton, who had lost his hold upon his constituents, and that of the Chicago capitalists headed by Douglas, whose power had already eclipsed that of both Cass and Benton. Douglas was preëminently a representative of the "moneyed classes" and his purpose was to build railroads from Chicago westward and northwestward which should tie to that growing town the great "back-country" of Iowa and the Nebraska territory then embracing hundreds of thousands of square miles. It was a long and bitter struggle between the two cities and the outcome depended on the turn of national policy—whether votes could be found for giving aid to the contemplated roads and whether a Pacific railway could be made to unload its enriching commerce in Chicago or St. Louis.

Since 1847, Douglas had been a railroad statesman, his first essay being the Illinois Central and the Mobile and Ohio, for both of which he had obtained rich grants of public lands from congress. These two roads connected New Orleans and Chicago and united more firmly the lower South and the Northwest, already tied together by the Mississippi. Having won the initial fight he thought in 1854 to "carry" the infinitely greater scheme, the Pacific railway with its eastern terminus at some point on the western border of Iowa which meant that Chicago would be the real

JEFFERSON DAVIS

winner. The forces which Douglas must unite were the same which had supported his Illinois Central-Mobile and Ohio program of 1850,[1] the middle West, the lower South and New York commercial interests.

The South was devoted above all else to slavery and the New York democracy was handmaid to this Southern interest. The old Benton group had been overshadowed in Missouri by the Atchison pro-slavery party. To unite these elements of the national economic life in support of his plans, Douglas must resort to some finesse for which he was eminently qualified. What the Gulf states demanded in 1854 was the expansion of the area of slavery and the consequent increase of her power in congress. This idea, too, was also exceedingly popular in the old South, in states like Virginia and North Carolina, and the Whig party in Kentucky was fast coming to the same position; Atchison's following in Missouri was about to overthrow Benton on a pro-slavery issue and was consequently half ready for coöperation with the lower South.

[1] Johnson, A., *Life of Stephen A. Douglas*, 166-176.

New York railroad men and capitalists required only profits. Douglas was willing to satisfy all these demands.

Davis's scheme for a Pacific railway was, of necessity, based upon the assumption that its eastern terminus would be Memphis, and its adoption by congress depended upon whether the former Benton following could be won. Davis expected to win this party through Atchison, for Atchison and Davis were intimate friends and ardent pro-slavery Democrats. Senator Jones of Iowa had been a schoolmate of Davis at Transylvania University in 1821 to 1824 and they were on the best of terms; the two Dodges, both senators, one from Iowa, the other from Wisconsin, were also friends of long standing. Davis counted therefore on winning the debatable ground of Missouri and Iowa for his undertaking, granting to St. Louis a branch line connecting that city with the far West, thus in reality offering to divide the eastern terminus of the proposed road. The President joined the Mississippi leader and called the attention of congress in his message of December, 1853, to the important subject and at the same time reported the annexation of the Mesilla valley region—a cession of territory from Mexico for the very purpose which Davis had in mind.

Douglas had not been idle. As chairman of the committee on territories he offered in the Senate on January 4, 1854, the bill which was to revolutionize the politics of the time. Douglas had been interested in creating a new territory west of Iowa many years. This interest in 1854 was as before largely dependent upon the expectation of building the Pacific railway which should terminate on the western border of Iowa, connecting there with Chicago roads. Thus two great plans of expansion and westward development were presented to the country almost at the same time. In order to win the South, Douglas finally changed his bill so as to open the Kansas end of the Nebraska territory to slavery. This secured Atchison at once, who had already been endeavoring to amend the Missouri compromise law so as to admit slavery into territories north of a parallel of 36° 30′; it won strong Kentucky support and enthusiastic approval throughout the

South. The great railway scheme behind Douglas's efforts was not broached; but from the evidence now available I think it hardly open to successful dispute that his major interest was in the building of the railway. The concession to the South on the point of slavery extension was not to Douglas very important, not comparable to the building of a railroad which would call into existence a line of prosperous communities all the way across the continent and make of Chicago the greatest city of the West. That Atchison and his friends would control Kansas and practically name the early delegates in congress was not a matter of concern to him, for was it not all inside the Democratic party?

No one was more surprised at the sudden upheaval which followed the introduction of the Kansas measure than its author and he never freed himself from the delusion that the excitement was due to the machinations of Chase and Sumner. Of course Douglas could not go before the people and say his object was the development and expansion of the middle West, and it would have been equally unwise to say that the South could not in the nature of the case profit from the measure.

But while the Douglas plans did not prosper Davis was completely checkmated by a leader of his own party, at the very outset of his second political career. The angry discussions in congress and the flaming popular resentment in all parts of the North served to show him that the South was in danger and that some increase in the number of Southern states was absolutely necessary if he and his friends were to continue to control the legislation of the country. His railroad plans were therefore the more important —so important that he made up his mind not to allow any other than a Southern Pacific line to be established. He counted on the power of the South, upon the favorable attitude of the majority of the Senate and upon the real advantages which he was certain would be offered by a survey of the route by way of southern New Mexico. But the bold secretary of war was predestined to defeat; he was never able to secure a favorable vote even in the friendly Senate though at the close of the Pierce administration he took up the cause in that body himself. Neither was Douglas able, after the blighting effect of his Kansas-Nebraska bill, to secure a favorable decision upon his major measure. The Gulf states were neutralized by the influence of the upper Mississippi region and nothing was done until a new régime came to power.

But Jefferson Davis did not return to his former position, that of 1850. He served his country as secretary of war with whole-hearted enthusiasm though it must be said that he never lost sight of the interests of the South. The army was enlarged, improved guns were introduced, young officers were sent off on various surveying parties for their better training, and the youthful George B. McClelland was sent as a special representative of the war department to observe and study the movements of the British and Russian armies in Crimea. Robert E. Lee, his boyhood friend, was made superintendent of the West Point Academy and Albert Sidney Johnston was advanced to important command; camels were brought from Arabia and assigned to the western army posts in the hope that they might be used in transporting military stores across the western deserts. The war department was alert and active while the future confederate president was in charge, and an examination of many personal letters received by him during that time has revealed no proof that he was preparing the way for future movements. He was a nationalist now and as a nationalist planned "large things."

It was upon his advice as well as upon that of Caleb Cushing that Townshend Harris and Commodore Perry were sent to Japan in the interest of American trade; that the attention of the country was called to the importance of the Panama canal project and the Clayton-Bulwer treaty negotiated; and that the purchase of Cuba from Spain was insisted upon by both Pierce and Buchanan. Davis was the true imperialist who believed that the borders of the United States ought to be expanded in all directions, that no weak and maudlin sentiment about the rights of weaker nations and the Declaration of Independence ought to prevent the American government from advancing to a position of power and influence in the world. Still it was the South which was to rule this imperialist republic, the South whose leaders were experienced statesmen and diplomats, and not the fickle and uncertain Northern democracy imbued with notions of equality, universal suffrage and free discussion.

In these policies he enjoyed the enthusiastic support of Mississippi, the most aggressive expansionist state in the Union during the years just preceding the civil war. Alexander G. Brown, a leader of little less importance in the lower South than Davis himself, was calling for the forcible seizure of Central American states in order that Southern institutions might be carried there; he, too, desired the Panama zone in order that our "shore line" might be extended on to California and next he would have reasoned, with eminent publicists of to-day, that all communities within our "shore lines" by a sort of manifest destiny belonged to the United States.[1] Other Mississippians and other Southerners dreamed dreams about American greatness very much like those of the present time; no wonder Davis was an imperialist and that he desired to

[1] Hart, A. B., *Actual Government*, 273-276.

annex all Mexico and planned to extend the Cotton Kingdom over the new region.

III

The administration of Buchanan was one long struggle of the South, which then dominated the Supreme Court, the United States Senate and controlled the cabinet, to make sure its power in the nation. The Democratic party was the great conservative organization through which the leaders of the South acted. The Democratic party was dominated by the South and the South was absolutely subordinated to her one great economic interest, slavery. The South was "solid" on that subject. No newspaper could thrive in that broad region unless its editor defended the institution, no preacher could hold his congregation who failed to do homage to the one supreme power which made and unmade public men at will, no professor was allowed to teach in any college if he dissented from the view of the planter class on slavery.[1] The legislative, the executive and the judicial powers of all the Southern states were in

[1] At William and Mary College, University of North Carolina, and Murfreesboro College, Tenn., examples were made of men who opposed slavery, 1856-1860.

the hands of men who owned slaves just as all these functions of most of the Northern and Eastern states to-day are dominated by the corporations and the monopolistic interests of the North.

But this united South governed by its trained statesmen and men of affairs did not control a majority of the votes of the Democratic party; more than half of the support of the party came from that great region then known as the Northwest, to-day the middle West. The man who could deliver this section to the Southern leaders and guarantee success at the polls in 1860, was Stephen A. Douglas, supported by the commercial, the speculative and especially the railroad interests of the upper Mississippi states; and Douglas was himself the master of a hundred slaves. The associates and lieutenants of Douglas in the Northwest were Governor Wright of Indiana, Jesse D. Bright, a Kentucky slave-owner, who represented Indiana in the United States Senate and James Shields, senator from Minnesota but at the same time representative of the Illinois Central railroad. One other senator from the Northwest who would go farther, perhaps, in aid of the South than any of these was George W. Jones of Iowa of whom Henry A. Wise wrote to Secretary John B. Floyd: "He is as good a nigger man as you or I."

The leaders of the South were Jefferson Davis, Howell Cobb, R. M. T. Hunter and Henry A. Wise, all but one heads of the chief committees in the United States Senate. Davis was the ablest, the purest, the wisest of this group and all Washington official life deferred to him during these last palmy days of the ante-bellum South. The senator from Mississippi was indeed Calhoun's successor. He spoke for the South as could no other, and like Calhoun, he was the representative of property, of the "interests" not of the struggling masses of common mankind who had adored Jefferson. Davis did not now believe in secession; but he counted on being able to govern the nation through the great powers of the Senate. It was not then, as it is not now, the interest of powerful property holders to break up the government and none saw this more clearly than Davis.

Looking carefully over the nation he found a

large minority in New York and Pennsylvania so devoted to Democratic tradition that it would have required an earthquake to shake their allegiance, just as we find in the same region to-day a hide-bound devotion to the Republican party as such. Tammany Hall, under the control of Fernando Wood, who was soon to become Mayor of New York, assisted by the wealth of August Belmont and Cornelius Vanderbilt, was then as now ready to do the bidding of the strongest group in the Democracy, which was the South. Besides, all the vast and growing patronage of the federal government was in the hands of the South for distribution. The tariff had been adjusted so that the hungry business interests of Pennsylvania looked to the party of the South, and not that of Seward and Chase, for further favors. The Supreme Court as already indicated was composed of slaveholders and men who lived in the North, but who might have lamented that they had not been born south of the Mason and Dixon line in order to enjoy the blessings of "the institution." The lawyers and planters who sat on that august bench were men who had been trained in the school of conservatism; their very mental processes served them well in their search for reasons and precedents to sustain the dominant interests of the time. There was little likelihood that a change in the character of that body would occur in a decade.

Well aware that these great points in the game gave him more than even chances against the insurgent North, Davis gave his thoughts to the affairs of the Buchanan administration in which he was almost, if not quite, as powerful as he had been when he was actually a member of the cabinet. He was consulted on all important questions; he read and improved presidential messages to suit his wishes; he dictated most of the foreign policy of the country and devised measures for the further aggrandizement of the South, confident that his section and his great "interest," slavery, would not be thrust from the seat of the mighty for years to come.

The purchase of Cuba, that "pearl of the Antilles" which had so long dangled before the covetous eyes of American statesmen, was a prime object of Davis and his close co-workers, Benjamin and Slidell, senators from Louisiana; the break-up of the Mexican Republic was encouraged and planned in the mission of John Forsyth to Mexico;[1] and the making of Kansas a slave state was expected as a result of Robert J. Walker's appointment to the governorship of that unhappy territory. These were large undertakings; but they were hardly less likely to be accomplished than had been the annexation of California, the settlement of the Oregon question, the passage of the Walker tariff and the reorganization of the finance of the country all during the stormy years of Polk's administration. The party was then new in office; it was, in 1857, old and thoroughly entrenched. In 1845 the great conservative Whig party was still in existence; in 1857 the opposition was made up of the rank and file of the common people with mere idealists for leaders—such for example as the Democratic situation offered in 1897. If ever the great moneyed and conservative interests of the nation held full sway it was during the four years just preceding the

[1] Callahan, J. M. Paper read before the American Historical Association at its recent meeting in Indianapolis, December, 1910.

civil war—and none knew this better than Jefferson Davis, before whom Buchanan is said to have trembled on more than one occasion.

But there was a cloud in the heavens scarce larger than a man's hand; it rose from the lake region of the Northwest. Douglas was not satisfied and Douglas was a "power" in the Democratic party. Robert J. Walker, the former Mississippi "boss,"—the man who had brought Jefferson Davis into public life during the exciting Polk campaign fifteen years before—was not satisfied to do the bidding of the Buchanan-Davis-Cobb political junta in Kansas and deserted the Southern leaders with whom he had acted since he became an ardent champion of the cause of Texas annexation in 1836. Walker sustained the free state party in Kansas and returned to Washington in the autumn of 1857 to win the President's approval or to resign his office and appeal to the Democratic masses of the North—the insurgents of the time—for vindication. Buchanan repudiated Walker, and the latter resigned; Davis denounced the "traitorous" governor who came to the capital pleading the cause of men who enlisted under the banner of John Brown of Osawatomie. The South was disgusted; the man who had led or prodded Polk into his war with Mexico and asked for the dismemberment of that unfortunate republic in 1847, largely on behalf of the pro-slavery interests, was now unwilling to make Kansas a slave state!

But Douglas took up the cause of Walker and on December 9, 1857, delivered one of his greatest speeches in the Senate in defense of the "squatters" who claimed the right under his Kansas-Nebraska bill of three years before to settle the slavery question by popular vote and a fair count. Douglas had been meditating such a course some time. The work of Walker in Kansas had aroused much popular enthusiasm in the Northwest and Walker had consulted Douglas as to the proper policy in Kansas both on his way to his post and on his return to Washington in November. And Douglas, mindful of the party interests, had carried the matter to Buchanan before congress assembled and warned him not to make the fatal blunder of espousing the Lecompton constitution. All to no avail. Douglas indicated to the President that he should oppose the administration and received the threat that "no Democrat ever yet differed from an administration of his own choice without being crushed." To which he replied: "Mr. President, I wish you to remember that General Jackson is dead."[1]

Douglas was now once again the most popular man in public life. Three years before he had "sidetracked" Davis's scheme for a Southern Pacific railway and put the Democratic party in a most difficult position by the introduction of his Kansas-Nebraska bill; he had then tasted the bitter cup of unpopularity, had heard himself denounced in his home town, had been burned in effigy at a thousand bonfires. The South alone was pleased. Now he was applauded by the very men who had lit the torches of 1854; Horace Greeley proposed him for the nominee of the next Republican convention, while his own party in the Northwest, where men had found it difficult to defend him, rallied to him as never before. Douglas had broken the democratic element of

[1] Johnson: *Life of Douglas*, 328.

his party away from its aristocratic and reactionary moorings. Men like Davis looked on in anger and wonder at the audacity of the Little Giant who could neither be cajoled nor threatened into support of the regular wing of his party.

From December, 1857, until the count of the votes after the famous Lincoln-Douglas debates, Davis and Buchanan and John Slidell, with all the powers of the federal government at their command, waged a war upon Douglas which was heartless and inveterate in its intense bitterness. Postmasters who refused to join the administration party were removed from office and Republican candidates for the Illinois legislature, which was to choose a successor to Douglas, were endorsed by the Democratic president. Davis watched the fight from his summer resort in Maine and hardly knew which to condemn the loudest—Lincoln's "house-divided" speech or Douglas's Freeport doctrine. Both were to him treason, the one against the country, the other against the Democratic party, the party of government. To a Mississippi audience he said later that he only wished the two debaters might, like the famous Kilkenny cats, have killed themselves and thus have rid the country of the pest of such discussions.

When it was certain that Douglas would return victorious to the Senate in the winter of 1858, Davis seeing clearly the nature of the struggle declared that the next presidential contest would be decided in the national House of Representatives.[1] The Republicans would nominate Seward, the Democrats would divide, the insurgents naming Douglas as their standard-bearer and the Southerners selecting Davis or Yancey, or perhaps some border-statesman like Breckinridge. No one thought Lincoln would receive the nomination or, if nominated, the majority of the votes of the country. Thus stood things to Davis on the eve of the Charleston and Chicago conventions. The historic Democratic party had gone to pieces with all its great plans: expansion of the national boundaries, trade with the far East, a railway to the Pacific and the spread of slavery over the territories of the Northwest. One wing was South-

[1] *Press and Tribune,* Chicago, December 2, 1858.

ern, conservative, reactionary, supported by the wealth and respectability of the nation and buttressed by the Supreme Court; the other was democratic, progressive, relying for its success upon the votes of small farmers and mechanics and the unparalleled gifts of their leader, Douglas. Nothing was clearer than that two men, Davis and Douglas, summed up in their persons and their policies the ideals of the two factions of the party of the country even at that time and these two men occupied seats in the Senate. A battle royal between abiding forces was on, and no one is surprised to-day to read in the files of the Washington papers of 1859 and 1860 that the galleries of the Senate were crowded from day to day as the fortunes of the one side or the other rose or fell. The South must have the votes of the Northwest to win; Douglas must command a Southern following. This was true whether the coming contest was decided at the polls or on the floor of the House.

IV

Neither Davis nor Douglas expected that war would come as a result of the break between the leaders of the South and those of the Northwest. Calhoun had said in 1844 that the one thing for the South to unite upon was her property rights, her one great economic interest, slavery, but he had no hopes that such a union could be brought about; he did all that could be done to compel Southern men to stand together upon this single issue, but died in the belief that he had failed and without any idea that a great war would be waged by the South for these interests. Davis had agreed with Calhoun in 1850 and he was then ready to secede; in 1858 he had little thought of breaking up the Union. He said in Faneuil Hall in October, 1858, that the radicals of the East and the extremists of the South were to the great nationalist masses as flies upon the horn of the ox. There was no thought of disunion in any of the speeches he delivered in New England that year. What Davis really desired was the presidency, and if the election should go to the House, he had excellent chance of winning his desire. I cannot but think that if ever the Cushing papers now at Newburyport, Massachusetts, come to light, this will be shown and that both Caleb Cushing and

Benjamin F. Butler went to the Charleston convention in 1860 with this thought nearest their hearts.

Davis thought property rights, and slavery in particular, would fare much better under the national government than they would be likely to fare if secession and civil war followed defeat at the polls in 1860. In fact he published a letter in the Charleston *Mercury* on November 10, 1860, declaring against secession. And when in December, 1860, the Governor of Mississippi called a conference of the state's delegation in congress, Davis voted against taking any steps that might lead to a break-up of the Union. The Mississippi senator was absolutely sincere in his desire to avert war and when he had been made president of the Confederacy he exhausted every resource to bring about a peaceful settlement and even attempted a reconstruction of the Union.[1] It was not Davis's telegram to Beauregard on April 12, 1861, that caused the first shot to be fired, but the decision of four subordinates of Beauregard,

[1] Roger A. Pryor, who then urged war and who ordered the firing at Fort Sumter, confirms this view of the author.

members of the general's staff, Roger A. Pryor,
Louis T. Wigfall, S. S. Lee, of Charleston, and
Senator Chestnut, which set the dogs of war to
their bloody work. Davis authorized Beauregard
to fire upon the fort if Anderson refused to surrender; Beauregard said the same to these hotheaded subordinates; and Anderson replied that
he would surrender in two days. Pryor and his
associates did not report to the General, but,
thinking that Davis was trying to reconstruct
the Union and negotiate with Seward to that end
and that the chance of war was about to slip away
forever, they conferred together and decided to
give the signal to the gunners to fire—and war
began, and such a war![1]

This much to show Davis's attitude. His
people in Mississippi did not misinterpret his purpose in 1858. They said he had set his heart upon
the presidency, and this was not far from the
truth. He had also come to see what the South
would lose by secession. If we admit now that
Jefferson Davis was the spokesman of the South
and of the great property interests there, that he

[1] Conversations with Roger A. Pryor, December 30, 1909.

commanded the machinery of the Democratic party and that he did not aim at breaking up the Union—all of which I think just and fair admissions—what shall we say was his policy, for if he did not think clearly and peer into the future during the last days of the old régime, no one did.

One thing is certain. Davis did not misunderstand the meaning of the Lincoln-Douglas contest. Lincoln represented in that fight the healthy moral, even radical, forces which Bryan and others called into action in Chicago in 1896, that is, Lincoln stood for the rights of men as against the rights of property, for the Declaration of Independence as against the guarantees of the Constitution; he denounced a Supreme Court which declared that negroes had no rights a white man need respect and he believed that, if Davis's power continued, if the court was not reformed and the Democratic party defeated, slavery would gain a footing in the Northwest and the North might lose its very status in the nation—a belief not ill founded if we examine well the sources of information now available. These ideas of Lincoln and his followers the South feared, for the South no longer believed in democracy.

Douglas was nearer to Lincoln than to Davis. He insisted that the power of property in congress and in the country must be limited, that slavery must not be spread over the Northwest, that definite limits to Southern expansion had been set by climate and geography and he demanded that these limits be observed, for this is what his "popular sovereignty" meant if it meant anything. Douglas was a democrat even if property interests of the Northwest were behind him; he believed in popular government though he rode on private cars or "free passes" supplied by the railroads which he had aided. There was thus not a great difference between Lincoln and his antagonist; and Horace Greeley was not so far in the wrong as some people thought when he proposed Douglas for the Republican nomination in 1860; and the followers of Lincoln and Douglas were more alike than their leaders. All wanted to limit the bounds of slavery, all were disgusted with the haughty airs and overbearing conduct of the ruling element in the Democratic party; and but for the metes and bounds which generations of party distinctions and party dislikes set and had set in the Northwest in 1858, these warring elements would have united and given such a solid majority that secession might have been postponed indefinitely. But in 1858, as in 1908, the real forces of reform were held in check by their own party prejudices; so that overweening special interests and monopoly privileges which preyed upon the public were not brought to their proper places in the social order, and the cost to the country, immense as it was during the war which ensued, has not been estimated aright nor even realized.

It was not in the nature of things for Davis who occupied the position, say, of Senator Aldrich or Secretary Knox, to read the signs of the times aright. Property was born blind; privileged interests in America, as formerly in France, could not be curbed, it seems, without destruction, and destruction is costly.

The work, then, of the great senator from Mississippi, and Davis was a great man, during the winters of 1858-59 and 1859-60 was not in the Senate nor yet in the committees which he

JEFFERSON DAVIS

controlled, but in guiding and shaping the forces which met Douglas in the Charleston convention in April, 1860. To this end he lent a hand to President Buchanan, who also received aid and comfort of Wall street, of the high tariff forces in Pennsylvania, and of William L. Yancey, the Southern orator, who had set his heart upon breaking up the nation as it then was. The ablest minds of the country were enlisted on the side of Davis and the President: Howell Cobb, John Slidell, R. M. T. Hunter, Caleb Cushing, B. F. Butler, John C. Breckenridge and Jesse D. Bright were all engaged on the side, apparently, of the "biggest battalions" and much money was spent by these men on behalf of their program.[1]

In the Senate Davis re-read the Calhoun resolutions of December, 1837, and he undertook to make them the platform of the party and rule Douglas out since the latter could not subscribe to the doctrine, put forth by Calhoun twenty years before, that congress was duty and honor bound

[1] Slidell was reported by the newspapers as being "on the ground" at Charleston two weeks before the convention met and "spending money freely" for the reactionary element of the Democratic party.

to protect property (slavery) in the territories, all territories north as well as south of the line of 36° 30'. These resolutions were supported by the "regular" wing of the Democracy and debated from week to week just before and after the assembling of the Charleston convention. The whole purpose of Davis was to make the strongest case possible for slavery, rally the greatest number of followers and give his representatives in the Democratic national convention all the moral support that he could command. Davis and the administration thus said to the country that the United States was not a nation, but a league of states, which was probably true; that congress, the agent of the independent states, was compelled under the constitution to protect slavery—all property recognized in any state—wherever it might go, which was also true; that the federal courts must thus interpret congressional action, and that laws of individual states, which in any way connived at the escape of fugitive slaves, were revolutionary.[1]

---

[1] These resolutions will be found in the *Congressional Globe*, 36th Cong. 1st Session, February 2—March 1, 1860.

JEFFERSON DAVIS

The South demanded the recognition of this "new Calhounism" as the doctrine which the country must accept, the alternative, in the minds of men like Yancey of Alabama and Rhett of South Carolina and A. G. Brown of Mississippi, being secession. Davis thought that might be a lawful alternative, but he was not ready to resort to it. He expected as yet to bring the Northwest to take his view or to expel Douglas, the exponent of the Northwest, from the party which would be equivalent to putting three parties into the field, the strongest of which would be that of the administration and the South. The outcome, as almost all politics showed, would be a repetition of the situation of 1825. If he were right in his view the "regular" nominee of the Charleston convention would be the next president and if secession were resorted to it would be New England, not the South, which would make the move.

It was also distinctly the policy of Henry A. Wise, 1858 and 1861, to hold fast to the federal government, thereby forcing the Abolitionists and the Republicans to make war for the possession of the capital in case of the failure of the Democrats in the elections of 1860. Wise said many times that he would never surrender the government which "Virginia had created," that he would punish Abolitionists as the authors of all the trouble. Who was dissatisfied? the South? No, the radicals of the North and East, who declared the Constitution "a league with hell and a covenant with the devil," were the complainants; they warred upon the Supreme Court, upon the states, upon the existing order, and they should be punished; they deserved the treatment of traitors.[1] This was the view of many slaveholders, of former Whigs and wealthy Democrats like Joseph Davis of Mississippi who knew what risks property owners would run if they followed Yancey and Rhett into the untried path of secession and independence. Jefferson Davis, as spokesman of Mississippi, did not so openly express this opinion, but there is little reason to doubt that he concurred substantially with his brother.

When the Charleston convention failed to

---

[1] Letter to George W. Jones, July 27, 1857. In Iowa State Historical Society collection.

nominate either Douglas or a follower of Davis and adjourned to meet again in Baltimore in June, 1860, Davis was still of the opinion that the South might win. Only late in the summer after two Democratic "tickets," led by Breckinridge and Douglas, had been put into the field, did he come to think Lincoln's election likely; then he went to Douglas and offered to withdraw Breckinridge and even Bell—the border states candidate—if Douglas would also withdraw from the canvass. Douglas could not yield for, as he said, most of his followers in the Northwest would then support Lincoln who, strange as it may appear, had become as conservative as Douglas and whose managers were declaring every day that slavery would not suffer if the great Illinois Republican came to power. It would be interesting indeed to know what passed between the bitter rivals and enemies on that September day. One wonders to-day whether some Eastern senator or political manager could thus propose and promise changes in the candidates of great parties, though the nation of our time is not the republic of 1860. However that may be, Davis, defeated in his plans, retired to his plantation in Mississippi to vote, await the returns and to give counsel to the lower South. It has been seen already that he published his opposition to secession in the Charleston *Mercury* after Lincoln's election was conceded, that he later advised the governor and the people of Mississippi not to secede. In fact he returned early to Washington to help Buchanan write his message, to discuss with Major Anderson, then stationed at Charleston, plans of improving and enlarging the Military Academy at West Point where he had spent some time during the summer with Anderson, ascertaining the needs of their beloved *Alma Mater*. This was not the attitude of one who was preparing to break up the government or to launch his craft upon the stormy sea of revolution. Davis did not think in November or in early December that the South ought to withdraw from the Union. He hoped to control the course of events, or to submit to the incoming administration if his friend Seward, who was thought to be the master mind in the rival party, retained power. Davis knew that Seward was himself the owner of slaves and he never had held him a sincere man. Why should not Seward give the South, especially the large conservative element there, what was demanded? Seward despised Lincoln, though he had agreed to sit in the new cabinet, and it was not at all improbable that he would bargain with the "interests" as most other statesmen of the North had done. As a representative of his class and of his people, Davis would not thus have sacrificed any trust or violated any of the assumptions of his high station. And this view of his position is confirmed by a contemporary document preserved by Henry Adams and recently published.[1]

Up to December 25, there was every reason to believe that the great pro-slavery party, with its vast wealth at stake, its prestige and its actual power in question, would win from the representatives of the new party the sort of promise which had been expected from Taylor in 1850 and which Clay gave, through Fillmore, as soon as "old Rough and Ready" was in his grave—that is, a

[1] *Massachusetts Historical Society Proceedings*, XLIII, 661.

promise not to interfere with slavery in the states and to allow the extension of the line of 36° 30′ to the Pacific, which would have meant the return of the South to power in 1864 and another slave state in southern California. Seward was willing to grant this, the older Whig-Republican leaders would gladly have averted secession with such a compromise. Lincoln alone refused to make any bargain, though it may safely be assumed that had he foreseen what was in store for him and the country he, too, would have yielded and the "interests" would have secured another lease of power.

The party of Jefferson had thus been transformed from an organization of small farmers and backwoods men, idealists in governmental theory, believers in the Declaration of Independence, to one which was dominated by the "interests," one whose dealers enjoyed special privileges in the state and who could wield the whole weight of Southern opinion and power in Washington without losing the support of the loyal masses at home. As parties grow old they, like governments, abandon their idealism, become absolutist in theory as well as in practice. The Jefferson party was no exception to the rule notwithstanding the heritage of its founder. Before the first Republican president had served out his second term his followers in Virginia were urging the Southern Federalists to join their ranks and promising the greatest possible security to slave property. When Calhoun came to leadership in congress he was not sure what attitude to take, and in 1820 he approved the policy of restricting the area of slavery; but in 1833 he became an extreme protagonist of this form of property. Thomas Ritchie, a true Democrat in the first part of his career as an editor and leader of Virginia, was for a long time an anti-slavery man at heart and was about to cast the weight of his great paper, the Richmond *Enquirer,* into the scales of the emancipation party in Virginia in 1831. For some reason he took definitely the pro-slavery view, and the Democratic party in the state of Jefferson became the party of slavery, rivaling the national Republicans who, as the party of the gentry, had been pro-slavery from the beginning, despite their strong affiliations in New England.

From Calhoun to Jefferson Davis was a long step. Slavery, as a blessing to the South and the world, was the parent of slavery, a divinely established order for which all true Southerners must take up arms. Yet Calhoun, Ritchie and Davis all claimed to be the followers of the author of the Declaration of Independence. The party which chose Buchanan and sustained his administration, which outlawed Douglas and repudiated Walker in Kansas, was the party which had been based upon a program of reform, of broad human rights, of anti-slavery ideals, a half century before. Great men who gloried in the Dred Scott decision honestly thought themselves followers of the man who attacked the Supreme Court of Marshall's day as "sappers and miners of the Constitution." "A negro has no rights which a white man need respect" was not a doctrine which could have emanated from Jefferson.

Thus far had property rights and a privileged status in the nation brought many of the ablest men of that generation, and to such extremes special privilege and great wealth lead to-day as certainly as in 1860. The only essential difference between the magnates who exploit the resources of the country and rule the Senate in 1911 and their predecessors of 1861 is the lack of a general belief in a doctrine of states rights which would justify secession. Davis acted, when he failed to negotiate in 1860 a tacit treaty with Seward, in the same way that many another Davis of our time would act if there were any appeal to a friendly but inflamed public mind. There was talk of secession in 1896 in cities which poured out their blood to suppress the cause of the South in 1860. Jefferson Davis only acted with his class when he laid down with much dignity and dramatic effect his senatorial robes in 1861 and journeyed sadly toward his Southern home. Perhaps most of us would follow in his footsteps, if we could to-day, rather than sacrifice great wealth and a privileged position in society.

INDEX

INDEX

ADAMS, J. Q., 110, 112.
ALLEN, WILLIAM, Senator from Ohio, 157.
ATCHISON, DAVID, of Missouri, 199, 202.

Baptists, 14, 21, 54.
BARRY, WILLIAM T., 123.
BEAUREGARD, P. G. T., 220.
BELL, JOHN, of Tennessee, 191.
BELMONT, AUGUST, 210.
BENJAMIN, JUDAH P., 211.
BENTON, THOMAS H., 159, 186.
BERRIEN, J. M., 123.
BEVERLY, WILLIAM, 6.
BIRNEY, JOHN G., 82.
BRANCH, JOHN, of North Carolina, 123.
BRECKINRIDGE, JOHN C., 235.
BRIGHT, JESSE D., 208, 225.
BROWN, ALEXANDER G., 184, 206, 227.
BUCHANAN, JAMES, 216.
BUTLER, BENJAMIN F., 220, 225.

CALHOUN, JOHN C. Parentage, 92; early schooling, 93; in college, 94; marriage, 97; in congress, 99; as a "Young Republican," 101, 104; internal improvements and the tariff, 107; in the cabinet, 109; first aspirations for the presidency, 112; defeats tariff bill 1827, 114; the South Carolina *Exposition*, 116; break with Jackson, 119; 124; nullification, 129; in the Senate, 131; a nationalist, 134; attitude toward slavery, 135, 139; opinion of Dew, 137; supports Van Buren, 138; efforts to unite the South and West, 140, 162, 219; aspires for nomination 1844, 142; in Tyler's cabinet, 144; Memphis speech, 148, 149; its reception at the South, 152; return to Senate, 154; Texas and Oregon, 155; Ten Regiments bill, 157; opposition to Wilmot proviso, 159; death and subsequent influence, 164.
CAMPBELL, WILLIAM, 26.
CARR, DABNEY, 20.
CARTER, JOHN, 7.
CASS, LEWIS, 157, 159, 186, 188.
CHASE, SALMON P., 202, 210.
CHEVES, LANGDON, 102, 114.
CLAY, HENRY, 85, 99, 102, 105, 109, 110, 115, 117, 127, 131, 132, 134, 141.
CLARK, GEORGE ROGERS, 27.
COBB, HOWELL, 209, 225.
COOPER, THOMAS, 114.
CRAWFORD, WILLIAM H., 85, 110, 113, 119

CUSHING, CALEB, 192, 195, 205, 220, 225.

DAVIS, JEFFERSON, 66, 152. Parentage, 173; education, 176; marriage, 178; cotton planter, 179; in congress, 181; lieutenant of Walker's, 184; in Mexican war, 185; in the Senate, 186; favors annexation of all Mexico, 156, 187; Southern policy, 188; supports Cass against Taylor, 188; debate with Foote, 191; in Pierce's cabinet, 192; personal appearance, 193; Southern Pacific scheme, 194, 195, 200; checkmated by Douglas, 198, 203; begins reforms in War Department, 204; imperialist, 205, 206; succeeds to Calhoun's leadership, 209; advisor of Buchanan's, 211; denounces Walker, 213; opposes Douglas, 216, 225; hopes of presidency 1860, 218, 219; opposes secession, 220, 230; retires to Mississippi, 230; hopes for compromise from Republicans, 231; resigns from Senate 1861, 235.
DAVIS, JOSEPH, 228.
DEW, THOMAS R., 81, 136.
DODGE, A. C., of Wisconsin, 148, 200.
DODGE, HENRY, of Iowa, 148, 200.
DONELSON, A. J., 145.
DOUGLAS, STEPHEN A., 148, 194, 197, 201, 208, 213, 223, 229.

EATON, JOHN H., 123.
Embargo, The, 61, 66.
EVERETT, EDWARD, 85.

FOOTE, HENRY S., 184, 191.
Force bill, The, 133.
FORSYTH, JOHN, 212.

GADSDEN, JAMES, of South Carolina, 148
GALLATIN, ALBERT, 51, 57.
GILES, WILLIAM B., 75, 78, 137.
GREELEY, HORACE, 223.
GRUNDY, FELIX, of Tennessee, 99, 105.
GUTHRIE, JAMES, of Kentucky, 197.

HAMILTON, ALEXANDER, 44.
HAMILTON, JAMES A., 119.
HARRIS, TOWNSEND, 205.
HARRISON, WILLIAM HENRY, 141.
HENRY, PATRICK, 4, 14, 15, 16, 19, 26, 27, 38, 47.
HUNT, RANDALL, 138.
HUNTER, R. M. T., 209, 225.

Internal improvements, 107.

JACKSON, ANDREW, 65, 111, 112, 130, 132, 137.
JEFFERSON, THOMAS. Parentage, 3; education, 5; popularity at college, 8; begins practice of law, 10; marriage, 11; prefers farming to law, 12; Western sympathies, 18, 19; partisan of Henry's, 20; ideals of the party, 21; believer in democracy, 23, 31, 33, 55, 73; in Continental Congress, 29; member of Virginia legislature, 32; breaks with Henry, 35, 41; in Congress 1781, 37; minister to France, 39; returns to Virginia, 43; organizes new party, 46, 48, 54; vice-president, 50; unpopularity in office, 51; elected presi-

INDEX

dent, 57; non-partisan, 59; Louisiana Purchase, 59; the Embargo, 61; hostility to the Virginia constitution, 67, 75; attitude toward slavery, 69, 71, 77, 79; opponent of Virginia court system, 71; favors a "recall" of legislators, 73; and wider suffrage, 74; efforts at reform, 76; last days, 82.
JONES, GEORGE W., 200, 209.
JOHNSTON, ALBERT SIDNEY, 204.

KIRCHEVAL, SAMUEL, 74, 75.

LAWRENCE, ABBOTT, of Massachusetts, 142.
LEE, HENRY, 49.
LEE, R. H., 6, 16, 19, 24.
LEE, ROBERT E., 204.
LEE, S. S., 221.
LEWIS, WILLIAM B., 118, 119.
LINCOLN, A., 221.
LOGAN, GEORGE, 51.
Louisiana Purchase, 59.
LOWNDES, WILLIAM, 102, 109.

MACON, NATHANIEL, 51, 57, 67, 71.
MADISON, JAMES, 20, 21, 46, 57.
MARSHALL, JOHN, 49, 52, 70, 75.
MASON, GEORGE, 19.
MASON, JAMES M., 162.
MCCLELLAN, GEORGE B., 204.
MCCLELLAN, ROBERT, of Michigan, 197.
MCDUFFIE, GEORGE, of South Carolina, 79, 94, 114, 127.
Methodists, The, 14, 54.
Memphis Convention, 148.

Nashville Convention, 163.
NICHOLAS, WILSON CAREY, 34, 83.

Nullification, 129, 137.

O'NEAL, PEGGY, 121.

PENDLETON, EDMUND, 26, 27, 36.
PETTIGRU, JAMES L., 94.
PIERCE, FRANKLIN, 192.
PINCKNEY, CHARLES, 58.
POLK, JAMES K., 146, 154, 157, 161.
PORTER, PETER B., of New York, 99.
Presbyterians, The, 14, 21, 54.
PRENTISS, SERGEANT S., 181.
PRYOR, ROGER A., 221.

QUITMAN, JOHN A., of Mississippi, 184, 185.

RANDOLPH, ISHAM, 3.
RANDOLPH, JOHN, 48, 130.
RANDOLPH, MARTHA JEFFERSON, 88.
RANKIN, JOHN, 82.
RHETT, ROBERT BARNWELL, 162, 227.
RITCHIE, THOMAS, 140, 143, 147, 152, 233.
ROANE, SPENCER, 21.
ROBINSON, JOHN, 16, 17, 18.

SCHURZ, CARL, 193.
SEDGWICK, THEODORE, of Massachusetts, 51.
SEWARD, WILLIAM H., 210, 217, 230.
SHELBY, ISAAC, 109.
SHIELDS, JAMES, of Minnesota, 208.
Slavery. Its growth in Virginia, 77; interstate slave trade, 78; the South and slavery, 134; 207, 234.
SLIDELL, JOHN, 212, 216, 225.
SMILEY, JOHN, of Pennsylvania, 102.
SMITH, WILLIAM A., of Virginia, 114, 138.

South Carolina. Exports 1810, 103; leads in congress, 103, 114; South Carolina *Exposition*, 116.
STEPHENS, ALEXANDER H., of Georgia, 191.
SUMNER, CHARLES, 202.

Tariff, The, 107, 114, 132, 134, 210.
TAYLOR, JOHN, of Caroline, 21, 67, 71.
TAYLOR, ZACHARY, 189.
TAZEWELL, LITTLETON W., 75.
THOMPSON, JACOB, 184.
TICKNOR, GEORGE, 85.
TRACY, URIAH, of Connecticut, 51.

VAN BUREN, MARTIN, 118, 138, 141.
VANDERBILT, CORNELIUS, 210.

Virginia. Exports 1810, 103; court system, 72; growth of sectionalism, 15, 16.

WALKER, ROBERT J., 144, 157, 181, 183, 185, 212, 213.
WASHINGTON, GEORGE, 49, 59.
WEBSTER, DANIEL, 151.
WELD, THEODORE, 82.
WIGFALL, LOUIS T., 221.
Williamsburg, Society at, 6, 7.
Wilmot proviso, 158.
WINTHROP, ROBERT, of Massachussetts, 142.
WISE, HENRY A., 185, 209, 227.
WOOD, FERNANDO, 210.
WRIGHT, JOS. A., Governor of Indiana, 208.

YANCEY, WILLIAM L., 162, 217, 225, 227.

Printed in the United States of America.